Susannah's QUEST

JOANNA STAUFFER

ISBN: 978-1-933753-720

Text design by Larisa Yoder
Cover design by Veritas Creative
Cover, Art, and Text Illustrations by Joyce Hansen

2673 Township Road 421
Sugarcreek, Ohio 44681

Carlisle Press   800.852.4482
WALNUT CREEK

Dedication

Susannah's Quest is dedicated to Susannah's grandchildren. Because you shared, her story lives on in these pages.

Acknowledgments

No book comes together without the help of many people. I'd like to name at least some of those who helped me piece together Susannah's Quest. It was a blessing to get to know you and an honor to work with you.

Alvin and Ruth Landis, Annie Gehman, Calvin and Josephine Stauffer, Earl Stauffer, Nancy Auker, Lucy Nolt, Lloyd Stauffer, Myles Parker, Elsie Stauffer, Arlene Stauffer, Annamae Auker, Irma Zimmerman, Ellen Sensenig, Lester Stauffer, Wayne Stauffer, Marvin Brubaker, Debbie Weaver, Melvin G Brubacher, (Elmira). All of you shared pieces to the puzzle. Thank-you for your help and every smidgen of memories you shared.

Friend Tracey Whaley, thanks for the hands-on spinning lesson! Your gift with that lost art amazes me.

Thanks to the Lorch family in May City, Iowa for letting me visit and explore your farm in May 2012. It helped me grasp a feel for the neighborhood and community that was once there.

Thanks to Kathy Mae Stauffer for tracing the pattern of Susannah's china onto paper. Part of that set of dishes is owned by Josephine Stauffer, who generously showed it to me.

Joyce Hansen, thanks for using your talents to grace the cover of this book.

To my family and close friends, you listened to parts of this story many times. Thanks for the encouragement and prayers.

To the folks at Carlisle Press. Several times I feared Susannah's Quest would never rise from your slush pile to see the light of day. Thanks for being the vessel who actually made that happen. Without editors and publishers, writers would merely be dreamers.

Last, but best of all, Jesus Christ, the author and finisher of our faith. Thank you beyond words for *your* life story, the one that never ends, which makes it possible that our own lives may end in a marvelous beginning with you. May Susannah's Quest bring glory to Your name.

Introduction

"We live in the present, we dream of the future, but we learn eternal truth from the past." This quote from L.M. Montgomery flashed through my mind frequently while I was working on Susannah's story. The truth of it resonated with the details of her life. There is much we could learn here.

You are holding a copy of her story in your hands because many people helped make it possible. Her story touched my heart in many ways. May it do the same for you. The God who provided for Susannah as a little girl, a young lady, and later a married woman is still the same God who watches over us today. With many prayers for wisdom on how to handle this story, I have attempted to keep it as real as possible. Minor character names have been fictionalized, however. Conversation is not original, for that would be nearly impossible. Minor details have been filled in to keep the story flowing. Bear in mind that some of the actual happenings in the story have neither the author's nor the publishers' approval in ethical matters. History isn't always rosy. Most of the contents of the story will be actual happenings shared with me by John and Susannah's grandchildren.

Significant research assistance was generously provided by Susannah's grandson, Alvin Landis. Special thanks to Alvin and Ruth for your time, your patience, and for freely sharing stories with me. The May City, Iowa, trip with the two of you was a blessing and a huge help. Without Alvin's vast historical knowledge, his copies of newspaper events during those years, and the generosity in sharing all that, this story wouldn't have become reality.

However, on my part, there may be mistakes on the coming pages. I ask the readers' forgiveness in advance for any discrepancies you may find.

Now unto him that is able to do exceeding abundantly above all that we ask or think, according to the power that worketh in us, unto him be glory in the church by Christ Jesus throughout all ages, world without end. Amen (Ephesians 3:20-21).

-J. Stauffer, Tunas, MO

Table of Contents

Prologue

"We married poor—and we're still poor," Mary Heckendorn muttered to herself as she stirred the pot of steaming turnips on the hearth fire.

The year 1878 was winding down and the chill of the approaching October night crept through the crack under the door. It was as if the draft curling slyly about the floor of the simple cabin wished to remind the woman that the oncoming Ontario winter would not be an easy one.

Mary had lived through forty-two winters. She well knew they were not for the faint of heart. Her husband John had proved a kind man in the years of their marriage. Kind, but slow, and more inclined to hunting and fishing than to working his way up in farming. When they'd married, John had been a day laborer, earning a mere pittance of wages. All these years and many moves later he was still working for others, with only a few possessions of his own. Settling the frontier in Ontario was hard, brutal work. Perhaps that was why John escaped to the woods and streams so frequently. For him, they yielded their bounty more willingly than the soil did.

It seemed their money could never be stretched far enough to make ends meet. To alleviate the situation, the oldest children were now living with other families and working for them for their room and board. But even without their ever-present appetites, there still wasn't enough food to reach around.

This week they'd gotten word of a family close to the village of Heidelberg who was looking for a young girl to be a companion for their only daughter in a family of sons. John had told Mary about it hesitantly. Upon her questioning he'd shared more information, and Mary realized he'd already made up his mind.

"You need Leah to help you here at home," he said quietly when she asked around the lump in her throat which one of the girls they'd send.

Mary knew she did indeed need ten-year-old Leah to help her with the work. Following a difficult pregnancy four years ago, baby Ezra had died the same day he was born. Mary's strength had never returned after the ordeal, nor had she been able to get over the grief of that sad day. Her heart still quivered at the thought of that tiny, cold body lying in a still colder grave, all alone.

Ezra was followed by Susannah, a lively dark-haired child full of mischief. Then there was Lydiann, the youngest.

"Which of the little ones will we send?" Mary asked her husband. "Did they say which one they preferred?"

"No. The choice is ours." John's eyes didn't meet hers. "We are to bring her along to the meetinghouse on Sunday. They'll take her from there."

The next few days passed in a blur, and now the week was nearly gone. Tomorrow was Sunday. Mary tried to keep her mind on preparations for the meager evening meal, but it was in vain.

At this moment the two little girls in question sat upon a log bench in the corner. Susannah's dark head was bent close to Lydiann's lighter tousles. They were intently playing with their rough corncob dolls.

A carefree giggle burst forth. Mary didn't have to look to see which girl's mirth had escaped. Nor did she have to see the sparkle in Susannah's eyes to know it was there. She knew it was nearly always present in the three-year-old's ebony eyes.

How was a mother to decide which of her two equally dear daughters to send away? Mary's heart was numb. The other girls had at least been older when they left home. She'd had them under her roof and under her protection longer, though the partings had never been easy. Then there was the separation with baby Ezra. But that had been the Lord's choosing. Though painful, Mary knew it was out of her control.

This was…Mary nearly groaned aloud. This was awful. If only John would say which one and take the decision from her shoulders—no, from her heart. Mary was sure her heart was being rent in two. Half would go with the girl that left, and the other half would bleed silently here at home with the girl who had lost her playmate.

This was the last evening her girls would be together. Mary decided to splurge and add a pat of butter to the plain turnips in the pan. The children would eat them better that way. Mary couldn't bear to think of her darlings eating their last meal together, but it had to be. Winter was fast coming on, and she knew neither their food nor their cash would last very long. Sadly, she tried to bolster her spirit with the hope that her daughter would be better cared for in someone else's home.

The door to the tiny cabin opened as John and the other children entered from doing the evening chores. A frigid gust of October night whooshed along in as if glad for the chance of an open doorway, rather than having to squeeze itself in through the many crevices with which the home was blessed.

A shuffle ensued as coats were shed, and soon the pegs along the wall were swaddled.

Mary lit the tallow candle in the hearth, shielded its spluttering flame with her hand, then lifted it high to the holder on the wall behind the table. Slowly she turned to fetch the pot of turnips from the heat. Placing the pot upon the handhewn lumber table she finally seated herself.

John and the children bowed their heads with one accord. Not for the first time Mary wondered with what words of thanks John addressed the Almighty for this scant meal before them. Her own mind could form no words of thanksgiving on this chill evening. Why could other families make a go of it, but they couldn't? Why must they always be moving from farm to farm, living in drafty shacks left behind by others who advanced to better and more comfortable living conditions? Would John even have work this winter? She knew once winter arrived in earnest, farms and any extra work became dormant, held in the icy clutches of brutal cold and snowdrifts.

John uttered a gruff, "Amen." Mary raised her bowed head and reined in her negative thoughts sharply. It wouldn't do to ruin the meal with circular reasoning which never provided answers, nor a change in circumstances.

She rose with ladle in hand to fill the tin bowls the children held out toward the steaming pot in their midst.

Noah's seven-year-old nose was keen. "Mother," he asked in anticipation, "did you put butter in the turnips tonight?"

"Yes," she replied, "I did."

"Yumm!" Leah cheered. "That makes them so much better!"

Mary ladled steadily. Tonight they would have all they wanted of this one dish upon her table. For, tonight, against her better judgment, she had tossed in four extra turnips.

"Um, good!" Susannah smacked her lips as she tasted the first spoonful. Even in the dim candlelight her eyes shone.

"Good! Good!" chirped Lydiann, wanting to add her voice to what seemed a festive air in her small world.

Mary only placed a half scoop onto her own plate. She was sure that would be all she could manage. For in her throat was a lump that felt as if she had already swallowed one of the vegetables whole.

The meal was eaten in near silence. The family was hungry. Casting weary glances around the table, Mary thought sadly, *Of our ten, we have only four here anymore. Nancy, Franey, Moses, Barbara, and Mary Ann are all living with others, working for their keep. And by tomorrow this time there'll be only three. Until the next one comes...* Mary knew that this last reason was why John felt it so necessary to thin the crop while they had the chance.

Since tomorrow was Sunday, baths needed to be administered yet tonight. Mary was glad for this extra action—grateful for one last chance to enjoy her small daughters. Glad too, that while she was busy with these tasks, her thoughts would have less opportunity to taunt her.

Later, once the little ones were tucked into the trundle bed alongside her and John's bed, in the small, chilly room off the main room, John asked what she'd been dreading all day.

"Have you decided which one yet?"

"No," she responded wearily. "How can I?" Her tone was sharper than she'd intended.

John sighed. "There's only one way I can think of."

"How?" Mary waited for more.

"Let's lay it before the Lord in prayer and let Him choose. Let it be the first one to come out into the kitchen tomorrow morning. That will be the one to go."

Mary absorbed this advice quietly. She saw at once the wisdom of John's advice. It would relieve each of them of the nearly impossible chore of deciding which one to give away.

"All right," she agreed slowly. "That's what we'll do."

Later that evening Mary's weary body lay upon the bed for a long time, tossing and turning, before her anxious thoughts finally quieted down enough to sleep. It seemed as though she'd barely closed her eyes before she heard John stirring. She opened gritty eyes. It was still dark, but he was indeed getting dressed for the day.

With a jolt she remembered what today was. Heart pounding, she sat up as swiftly as she could. Listening closely, she could hear the rhythmic breathing of the two little girls coming from the tiny bed upon the floor. Oh, they were still there! Both of them!

Relief was short-lived. She dressed numbly. Quietly she followed John from the room.

With a heavy cloud of dread pressing upon her heart she attempted to perform her morning duties.

John stirred the fire, trying to revive the spent embers. She could hear him adding kindling, as if this were any other day.

A soft rustle whispered at the doorway of their room. Mary froze. Above the beating of her heart she heard small footsteps running to John near the hearth.

When she could stand it no longer, she slowly turned to see which girl would be the one.

It was Susannah.

rah's Travels

St Jacob's

CHIGAN

NEW YORK

Snyder County

PENNSYLVANIA

A   OHIO

MARYLAND

WEST
VIRGINIA   St Mary's

ENTUCKY   VIRGINIA

Part I

MICHIGAN

St Jacob's

chapter 1

Living with the Martins
(circa 1885)

"Susannah, today you will watch the heifers and keep them out of the wheat field." This statement came from Mr. Martin's lips as the family congregated for breakfast on a Monday morning.

It was an ordinary assignment—one that Susannah had done many times before. It wasn't even such a bad chore. It was just that in spite of herself, ten-year-old Susannah had secretly hoped she would be one of the fortunate ones who might make the cross-country trek today to attend the new term beginning at Hollinger School.

Her thoughts now became stormy. Had it mattered to them, the Martin family could easily have read her thoughts by the set of her slender jaw and the scowl that brewed on her brow.

But the feelings of this youngster weren't a high priority to the family. Mr. and Mrs. Christian Martin ran their farm and family as efficiently as a millstone grinds raw wheat kernels into fine flour. The farm would flourish, no matter what it took to make that happen. If others' plans or hopes needed to be crushed to stay on schedule or to keep up appearances, so be it.

Susannah didn't hear the directions issued to the other youngsters around the table that morning. Not until the senior Martin barked an order to his youngest son.

"Christian, you will go to school this week."

Young Christian took the order without flinching. But when his eyes met hers, there was despair in them to match that which raged in her own bosom.

The irony of the situation did not escape the two. For Christy detested school as much as Susannah craved it.

For her it had been a welcome escape. The world of books, numbers, and facts opened up for her as amazingly as a wild rosebud opens in warm spring sunlight. But in the eyes of the Martins, schooling for girls was an unnecessary waste of time and energy. Yes, their only daughter, Betsy, had been sent to school, for she was a Martin. One of their own. And their sons, of course, must attend. They must be prepared to manage—and manage well—any farm or business that came their way. But Susannah wasn't one of their own. They were merely raising her.

Grudgingly they conceded that since they were now living in the 1880s, everyone should at least learn to read and do ordinary sums, so last year if no other duties had pressed too urgently, Susannah had been permitted to attend school until she was nearly through the second primer. Even so, her attendance had been sporadic. Often after her work was done in the evening she studied by candlelight to be able to keep up with her classmates.

She had hoped to be able to attend this term yet. But now, with Mr. Martin's order to watch the heifers, those hopes were flung out like a pan of dirty dishwater.

Thus it was that a short while later Susannah opened the door at the side of the large barn and herded six young heifers and the two milk cows down the lane and out to pasture. The morning air was brisk. Anticipation ran high among the beasts for a day of munching on lush green grass. Two took off at a lively trot, while the rest followed willingly. The leading heifer lowered her head and with a gleeful kick of her heels set the tone for a day that Susannah knew would keep her busy.

The Martin farm consisted of gently rolling land, much of which had been cleared from forest in recent years. Some of the pastureland still harbored too many stumps to be farmed efficiently. To such a strip of pasture alongside the wheat field Susannah now directed her charges.

At first the heifers were content to graze in their permitted area, but not for long. Soon the most adventurous one in the group decided she'd much rather taste the wheat alongside the pasture, for it was much darker green and surely more flavorful.

For a brisk half hour the slight Susannah ran to and fro, frantically establishing the boundary for the heifers.

She had just plopped down on a grassy knoll to catch her breath when young Christy came into view.

He was by now out of sight of the farmhouse, trudging to school with an expression of indifference on his young, round face. His lunch pail swung lazily from his lanky arm. At sight of Susannah, his countenance brightened, for here was a chance to tease her.

"Ha, just wait till I tell Father you just sit out here resting, and don't even watch the heifers," he began.

Susannah didn't answer. A retort would merely egg him on.

"You'll catch it then," he continued. "They might as well send you to school, as little as you do around here!"

Susannah rose to her feet, eyes flashing. As she bent to grab a dried cow pie to hurl at him, he continued.

"Yes, and now that wheat is worth $1.50 a bushel, you're really going to catch it when he sees what a mess they made in the wheat field." Christy pointed toward the bold heifer who by now was nibbling at the edge of the forbidden wheat.

Susannah's aim was excellent, and the cow pie hit Christy's shoulder, but it only bounced off, as did the words she flung at him. "Ya, and it's pretty useless to send you to school! You don't even learn much!" The reddening of his face was the only indication that her retort hit home, for indeed, he was the slowest learner of the family.

Knowing he'd soon be late for morning classes, Christy continued on his way.

For the next while Susannah was kept busy with the heifers again.

The two older cows soon knew it was useless to venture too close to the edge of the pasture, but the heifers wouldn't let Susannah rest.

"Ach, you want to go into the wheat field about as bad as I want to go to school, I'm sure," the girl muttered, as once more one of the herd tried her to the limit.

Finally she had a chance to rest again.

Then, in clear, deep tones on the morning breeze came the unmistakable "Bong! Bong! Bong!" of the school bell.

Susannah groaned, but uttered no wistful words to the heifers. It would do no good.

chapter 2

If Wishes Were Dishes

Susannah no longer remembered her own home life. For as long as she could remember she had been here with the Martins.

She knew, of course, that she was a Heckendorn and not a Martin. This fact was never kept from her; rather it was thrown into her face at every opportunity.

The Martin family consisted of the parents, Christian and Maria, and their seven children. Tobias was the oldest, followed by Isaiah and Joseph. Next was Elizabeth, who was called Betsy by all who knew her. Then came Reuben and Elias, followed by Christian, who was less than a year older than Susannah.

It was commonly known throughout the Mennonite settlement that John and Mary Heckendorn were poor—poor to the point that they couldn't keep their family together. Poor in everything, that is, but children, for of these they had eleven.

Susannah knew her own youngest brother, Israel, only from seeing him Sundays at the meetinghouse when he attended with her parents. This was also the only time she saw her parents. Some of her oldest siblings had by now married and started homes of their own.

"Why do people call my father Indian John?" Susannah asked Betsy one day as she helped her dig potatoes.

"Because he'd rather loaf around in the woods watching wild things," was Betsy's answer. "He doesn't like to work the land, like *my* father, or like the other Mennonite men. So he just works for other people, and whenever he feels like it he heads off to the forest. Like an Indian."

"Oh." Susannah digested this information. "What about my mother?" she asked next.

"Well, she's a good woman. But if her husband won't earn a decent living for them, what can she do? A dollar a day doesn't go far these days, with a family that size."

Susannah carefully placed more potatoes in the basket. She'd been sharply admonished not to bruise them. Bruised ones rotted quicker, and potatoes weren't a crop that produced well to start with. She surveyed the long row in front of them. How she hoped they could get most of them dug before Mrs. Martin and Betsy left with the team to go to St. Jacobs for supplies.

After they left, she'd be the only one to work on these long rows.

"And then your parents took me in." Susannah said this fact quietly, as if to close the subject in her own mind.

"Uh-hmm," Betsy agreed. "I always wanted a sister. All I had was all those boys. Once Mother was sure there would be no more girls, they decided to ask for one of you Heckendorn girls. I suppose your parents were glad enough to let someone take care of another one for them."

Susannah wished Betsy hadn't added that last sentence. It made her feel all tight and sore inside. *Did my parents really not want me?* she asked herself. *I wonder if my father really is lazy. I heard someone once say that he works hard enough when he does work.*

"Betsy! Come in now! Time to go!" The call interrupted Susannah's thoughts.

With a swift shake of her skirt and apron to rid herself of garden dust, Betsy turned to leave.

"You'd better go do the wash now, Susannah, so it dries for sure. Then you can dig potatoes until dark." With this, Betsy left.

A groan escaped Susannah. Slowly she followed Betsy, lugging the heavy basket of potatoes. It took her eyes a moment to adjust to the dim cellar. She placed the potatoes carefully into the slatted potato bin.

By the time she reached the back porch of the farmhouse, the team was rounding the curve of the driveway past the house. The sleek bay horses trotted in step, with Betsy confidently at the lines.

Susannah watched wistfully. She didn't expect a parting wave from either of the women—and she didn't receive one.

Bracing herself, she turned to hurry upstairs to change into her only other dress, so that she could wash this one. It needed to be clean to wear to church tomorrow.

This done, she gathered the other dirty laundry from upstairs and heaved it down the stairwell. Christy's shirt stuck to the top step. Susannah's bare foot shot out, and with a defiant kick she sent it sailing down to join the others on the heap.

Susannah lugged the oak washtub to the back porch, setting it squarely on its own bench. Then she fetched the washboard and soap. Carefully she carried hot water from the large black kettle, one pailful at a time. It seemed to take an extra lot to fill the tub today. Gingerly she tested the water temperature with the tip of her smallest finger.

"Oh! Still too hot!" she gasped. Grabbing the pail and running to the yard to the pump, she worked the long handle up and down until a stream of water gushed out. Adding this to her tub of wash water brought it to a temperature she could stand to work with.

She dipped in one piece of clothing at a time, letting it soak completely before she grabbed the slithery bar of soap and rubbed it vigorously across any stained areas. Then she scrubbed and rubbed the garment across the corrugated metal of the scrub board. A stream of dirty water seeped out of the cloth, running down over the board and into the tub.

There was time to think as Susannah performed this chore. *Just once I'd like to go along to buy supplies,* she thought. *But it's not likely to happen.* At least it never had happened. Always, always, there was work to do here at home.

A single tear slid slowly down her cheek and with a tiny plop it landed in the wash water. Had anyone been watching, it would have gone unnoticed anyhow, for the steamy water above which the girl worked had created a few beads of sweat on her forehead.

Will it always be like this? Susannah wondered. *Never a change for the better?* She knew that the others in her family didn't all get treated like this. Her sister Franey had once worked for the Jacob Brubaker family. Mrs. Brubaker was very kind to Franey. Every time she went to town she brought along a pretty china dish as a gift for her maid. The thought warmed Susannah's heart on behalf of her sister.

She straightened to stretch her aching back, then bent to add another dirty shirt to the tub.

It did no good to wish though. Susannah knew there wouldn't be a china dish along for her when the others returned from St. Jacobs later that afternoon.

chapter 3

Pioneer Pains

Winters in Ontario were long and cold. More white with snow than not. Both man and beast hunkered down at the beginning of the season and resigned themselves to a slower pace.

No season on the Martin farm was an idle one, however. Mrs. Martin was as thrifty as she was firm. Nothing went to waste. Let the winds howl and moan as they whistled around the outside of the home. Inside the large farmhouse she kept the fire blazing and the work going.

The floors were nearly always chilly, for this is where the drafts of the strong winds outdoors played out their strength once they'd slipped into the home.

Braided rugs dotted the floors, made from the worn garments of the family. The craft of making these rugs was a necessity, but also an art.

"Susannah, go up to the attic and bring down that stack of old clothes we took up last spring," came the order one winter day.

Susannah hurried. The large attic was so cold she could see her breath form a white fog. Grabbing the worn garments she returned to the fireside.

"You remember how I showed you last winter to rip the seams out, then cut strips and stitch them end to end?"

"Yes." Susannah well remembered that repetitious job.

"Well, start with that. Then I believe you are old enough to learn to braid them too this winter," Mrs. Martin said.

Susannah began. She was eager to learn to braid the rugs. Up until now she had chafed under the mundane chore of merely getting the strips ready for Betsy to braid.

Conversations while doing this work often swirled about the kitchen as freely as the snowflakes that flew outside. In the evenings after their stomachs were satisfied with a warm, hearty supper, Mr. Martin and his sons sometimes contributed to the talk.

"Father, tell us again how the plain people came to live here in Canada," requested Reuben one evening.

The tedious task of ripping seams, cutting strips, and sewing them together didn't require all of Susannah's concentration. She enjoyed listening to the stories of long ago and hearing of the adventures of the early pioneers.

"Well," Father Martin began slowly. "The Indians here were a big help to the British during the American Revolution. When the war was over, the British gave the Grand River Valley to the Indians in appreciation for their help."

The fire in the stove popped and snapped. Outside, the winds whooshed around the sturdy home. Susannah's ears were tuned to catch every word.

"What then?" asked Elias.

"Their leader was soon trying to sell the land because more and more white settlers were coming into the area. The Indians believed they could keep as much land as they needed for their tribal camp and planned to live many years off the money from land they sold.

"The government wasn't happy about that. They didn't want the Indians to profit from the gift of land. After a quarrel with the Indians, they appointed trustees to 'help' the Indians with the transactions. This proved disastrous for the Indians. They were swindled out of most of their money.

"The earliest Mennonites to arrive in the area came in the late 1700s. Land prices in Pennsylvania had gotten expensive and the Mennonites were wishing for more land to farm to support their families. The West was still wide open, but crossing all those mountains didn't appeal to them. They believed it was less dangerous to follow the mountain ridges north. They sent scouts first. Favorable reports reached them, and the first ones prepared for their move to Canada.

"The trip wasn't easy. Often a number of families traveled together in a caravan of about sixty people. The journey took twelve weeks or more. Young boys and men walked most of the way, driving the cattle.

"By 1801 a group from Lancaster County, Pennsylvania, arrived. With them was a young man named Samuel Bricker. He spent a year clearing land and building a cabin. In the spring of 1802 he went back to Lancaster and married Rebecca Eby. He also persuaded his brother John and several other families to move north with him. So another caravan of heavily loaded Conestoga wagons lurched and swayed northward. By that fall the young settlement in the Grand River Valley had 25 families.

"Trouble came when young Sam Bricker went to register his purchase of land in December of 1802. Then he learned that the land was heavily mortgaged, and the titles held by the Mennonite community were worthless!" Mr. Martin paused in the story.

"Then what?" Reuben asked. "Did they go back to Pennsylvania?"

"The settlers weren't the only ones upset with the deal," Mr. Martin continued. "The man responsible for the transaction with the Indians was five years behind in mortgage and interest payments. The government even threatened legal action against him. In the meantime, Sam and John Bricker went back to Pennsylvania to see if their elderly father would help them.

"He was too old and sick to take an interest in their problem, so the brothers went to their in-laws, the Ebys and Erbs, who were quite well-to-do. After several years of negotiations between the Mennonites and the government, they founded what they called the German Company. It was a business venture owned by shareholders, and the agreement was to pay the price of 10,000 British pounds to the Ontario government for this 60,000-acre tract. After several years, the tangled question of land ownership was finally settled here in Waterloo Township. The Mennonites had control of the German Company Tract at a price which was a bargain compared to Pennsylvania property.

"They began to build communities. John Erb built a sawmill and a gristmill at Preston. Sawn lumber was in great demand for the buildings of the new community. Abraham Erb went a bit farther north to Laurel Creek to build his sawmill and gristmill. Also, in these years, Benjamin Eby settled near where the town of Berlin (later Kitchener) would rise and began to teach school. In 1809, he was ordained a minister for the Mennonites, and a few years later he became the bishop for the Waterloo area. Both school and church services were entirely in German. The township's first meetinghouse was built near Eby's home.

"So then this area was settled slowly over the years. But those first settlers had years of hard labor to get to where we are now." Father Martin cleared his throat. "Many of them would be surprised at how soft we've become in the 70 years since then."

He stood and went to the stove, putting in another piece of wood to keep the fire blazing for a few more hours. "Time for bed, all of you," he ordered.

Mrs. Martin and Betsy laid aside the rugs they'd been braiding. Susannah rose from the floor where she'd been, sorting the strips of cloth she'd cut.

Carefully she moved them into the front room where they would be out of the way. Perhaps tomorrow she would be permitted to begin braiding.

Hurrying up the cold stairway to the bedroom she and Betsy shared, she shivered as another blast of wind shook the house. After preparing for bed as quickly as possible in the cold, unheated upstairs, Susannah lifted back the heavy woolen comforter and dived into the bed beside Betsy. Quickly she pulled the cover back up over her chin. She stretched out stocking-clad feet to reach the brick Betsy had warmed on the stove and placed in the bed for warmth to their toes.

Her thoughts were still on the stories they'd heard Mr. Martin telling them tonight. *How would it be to travel so many miles in a wagon?* she wondered silently.

Another blast of wind shook the house and she shivered. It almost felt as if even the bed were shaking from the strength of the cold wind outdoors! *Maybe that's how those Conestoga wagons shook and creaked on the long trip,* she imagined.

"I wonder how Pennsylvania looks, anyhow?" The question popped out aloud in the darkness of their bedroom.

"I don't know," Betsy answered. "I don't expect to ever see it. And you won't either. Now go to sleep." Her voice was muffled by the heavy cover.

Susannah snuggled down deeper. No, it wasn't likely that she would ever see how Pennsylvania looked.

chapter 4

Never Good Enough

This isn't as easy or as fun as it looks, Susannah admitted to herself. Her rug braiding lessons had begun. Instead of soon having a sizable portion to display, all she had to show was a lumpy mess.

"Here, pinch the end into the bureau drawer to start it off like this." Betsy tucked the end of Susannah's first braid into the side of the bureau, then closed the drawer. "Now, just pull gently as you braid, then it will stay straight and even."

Susannah began again. She gathered the strips and this time the unruly tangle became a smoother braid. First hold the deep green strip, then fold over the brown one, and with the other hand pull over the blue one.

"How long shall I make this?" Susannah asked.

"Oh, keep going," Betsy advised. "It needs to be quite long before you start lacing it together."

Susannah's fingers were so busy braiding that she forgot to keep an even tension on her braid. As she gave a jerk to untangle the brown strip, the end of the braid was tugged out from the bureau drawer and landed with a triumphant plop on the floor.

Mrs. Martin came into the kitchen at that moment. "Ach, Susannah!" she scolded. "How long will it take you to learn? Betsy learned right off!"

Susannah felt her face heat up. She didn't dare lift her eyes to meet

Mrs. Martin's face, knowing full well the exasperated expression that would be glaring at her. Angry thoughts churned through her mind. *Why am I always being compared to Betsy? It's not fair! Betsy is ten years older than I am! Besides, Betsy had to learn sometime too.* Susannah was relieved when Mrs. Martin left the room again.

With a sigh she bent to pick up the end of the contrary braid. She pinched it into the side of the bureau again.

Softly Betsy said, "It took me a while to learn too. I remember how hard it was."

Susannah shot a grateful glance at her. Betsy was a dear!

"Shall we sing?" Betsy asked a few seconds later.

"Yes, let's," Susannah agreed.

Betsy was old enough to attend the young folks' gatherings and had quickly learned the hymns they sang there. Now she often sang them here at home. How Susannah loved it when Betsy sang! Entranced, she listened as Betsy's clear voice rose to the highest notes, then skipped softly down to the lower ones.

"How about 'Lily of the Valley'?" Betsy asked. Then she began to sing.

This was one of Susannah's favorites. She lifted her own voice and joined in with the words she'd memorized from hearing Betsy sing it so often.

Susannah didn't understand all that the words meant, but the last verse was her favorite. The words seemed so strong and brave. Though she didn't really understand them, they were a comfort to her. "He will never, never leave me, nor yet forsake me here, while I live by faith and do His blessed will." Her girlish mind didn't grasp what "His blessed will" was, but she knew what it was to feel forsaken and unwanted. Then came the triumphant, "A wall of fire about me, I've nothing now to fear, with His manna He my hungry soul shall fill. Then sweeping up to glory to see His blessed face, where rivers of delight shall ever roll."

Betsy's voice rose for the refrain. "He's the Lily of the Valley, the bright and morning star. He's the fairest of ten thousand to my soul."

As the last notes echoed sweetly through the kitchen, Susannah's spirit longed to know the comfort of this friend Jesus of whom the song was about.

"Looks like you're ready to begin putting your rug together," Betsy said, interrupting Susannah's thoughts.

"What do I do next?" Susannah asked.

"Thread the bodkin, then I'll show you."

Betsy laid Susannah's long braid on the floor then Susannah knelt beside it. "Hold the braid flat with your one hand," Betsy directed.

Susannah sat cross-legged on the chilly floor. Under Betsy's watchful eyes she began to double the braided strand around itself.

"No, don't stitch *through* the braid," Betsy corrected. "Poke the bodkin *between* the folds of the braid, then draw it tight."

Susannah concentrated as hard as she could. As she rounded the curve of her infant rug she soon saw that the curves would be the hardest part. On this first one she had stitched the braid up so tightly that the edge buckled up stubbornly.

"That won't work," Betsy said. "It will trip someone. Take those stitches out and start over."

A soft groan escaped Susannah. "Ach, how long will it take me to learn this?" she muttered to herself, unconsciously repeating the words Mrs. Martin had scolded her with earlier.

Silently she resolved that her next attempt would not buckle up for her. She stitched the curve again, loosely this time.

That didn't look right either. This time there were loose gaps in it where the braid should have fit snugly against the first row.

"Here," Betsy offered. "Let me do the first round. The next ones won't be so hard. You can do those. Now watch."

Susannah bent forward to see better. Betsy's fingers deftly slipped the blunt-tipped bodkin between the sides of the braided cloth. Then she pulled it out and drew it tight. Between, pull, tight. Between, pull, tight.

It looked so easy when Betsy did it. Soon she was done with the first curve. She went along the straight side swiftly. Under Betsy's fingers the second curve was looped in place skillfully.

"Well begun is half done." Betsy spoke as one who'd had plenty of practice. "Why don't you try it again? The curves aren't so bad from now on."

Susannah grasped the bodkin again. Her fingers were damp with nervous perspiration. With one hand she held back the attaching braid to keep it flat. With the other she looped the strand of her thread through, attaching the braids side by side.

"How's this?" she asked cautiously.

"Keep going," encouraged Betsy. "It'll get better."

Susannah began the second round with more confidence. She noticed how the three colors of her strips now formed a pleasing pattern. The brown, green, and blue blended well. She'd never realized what went into the rugs that lay upon the floors, even if it had always been her job to gather them up and take them outdoors for a brisk beating on cleaning days.

Now the strips of worn cloth were finally responding to her touch. She felt a warm sense of accomplishment fill her heart.

Mrs. Martin came in from the porch just then. "Well," she remarked tartly. "Are you finally getting through to her, Betsy?"

Susannah met Betsy's glance.

"Yes," Betsy replied. "She's learning."

A warm circle of gratitude chased around Susannah's heart. Betsy's kind answer was a balm to her spirit.

chapter 5

A Broken Nose

Spring had come to the farm. It seemed no less than a miracle that the deep drifts of snow blanketing the farmyard and surrounding countryside were finally gone.

Susannah had forgotten how green things could be. It seemed everywhere she looked the bright new life of another season was beaming out upon the landscape. The tall pines, of course, had remained green all winter. But most of the time they had been wrapped in snowy, knee-length cloaks, making their few protruding needles look nearly black in contrast. Now, freshly watered with melted snow, and bathed in mild sunshine, they wore their traditional, dark piney green. In contrast, the new leaves of the maples and oaks were a paler, shiny green. The pasture sported the soft sheen of new blades of grass. All this blended together to create a verdant picture most pleasing to the young girl's eyes and spirit.

The air smelled fresh and pure. It held mixed notes of freshly plowed earth, pine needles, and newborn apple blossoms. It was a shame to waste such a day by being stuck indoors, but that was where Susannah found herself. Betsy had gone to the village with her parents.

There was something else in the air besides just spring—Betsy was getting married. Young Amos Martin had brought her home from the youth gatherings several times, and there was no doubt in Susannah's mind that he was serious. Betsy too, at nearly twenty-two years of age, saw no need to stall for time.

So the trip to St. Jacobs today was more than an ordinary run for necessities. Since Betsy still worked on the home farm, helping her parents, they were going to buy some household essentials for their daughter to set up housekeeping.

Betsy seemed excited and very pleased with the direction her life was taking. Susannah couldn't quite grasp the joy that radiated from her. What was so great about Amos? The little she'd seen of him certainly hadn't left her with any great enthusiasm for the young man. He seemed very ordinary, much like Betsy's brothers—someone to cook for, clean up after, and do laundry for. Why Betsy looked so forward to moving into a home with him after their marriage was more than Susannah could figure out.

She did realize that Betsy had changed. What had brought about this change Susannah couldn't put a finger on, but the last year had certainly mellowed Betsy. No longer did she, like her mother, hurl hateful comments at her. She had also become more patient when teaching her how to get her chores done more efficiently. How much it had to do with her upcoming marriage, Susannah didn't know. Maybe it was more a result of Betsy's baptism. Not much had been said about that, though Susannah gathered that it was an important step to be made. It didn't matter. She gladly soaked up the unexplained kindness from Betsy.

Mrs. Martin remained her usual self. Just today, prior to leaving for town she'd followed her long chore list for Susannah with a curt, "And don't be eating any of the new sugar while you're mixing the bread dough!"

Even now, as Susannah set about the task of soaking a portion of the hard yeast cake, her cheeks burned with shame and a good bit of anger.

Many a time she had seen Mrs. Martin place a morsel of the crusty brown maple sugar from the barrel into her own mouth. However, one day she caught Susannah sampling it, and one would have thought a serious crime had been committed.

Opening the barrel now for the half cup needed to add to the bread dough, Susannah quickly dipped out what she needed, then slammed the wooden lid back down. Should Mrs. Martin ask her later tonight, Susannah was determined to answer negatively with a clear conscience.

Setting the bowl of dough near the back of the wood stove, where the gentle warmth would help raise the dough, Susannah went about her other work for the day.

Many hours later she heard the clip-clop of the returning team. Sure enough, the wagon was loaded with a large dresser and many other boxes and bundles.

Elias and Christy were summoned. With exaggerated moans and groans the two moved the dresser into the front room at Betsy's direction. Susannah helped carry in other crates and bundles.

"Careful," Betsy cautioned. "That one has my new dishes in it."

"Dishes?" Susannah gasped.

"Ya. They bought me a new set of good Sunday dishes," Betsy said happily.

"Oh!" Susannah was excited as well. "May I see them?"

Mrs. Martin overheard. "You keep your hands off Betsy's new dishes! They're too expensive to be handled carelessly and broken!"

Susannah's face flamed. But she bit back a retort.

"When I get a chance I'll unpack a few," Betsy whispered behind her mother's stiff back. "Then maybe after chores you can look at them."

Susannah turned to go finish her work. There were still the chickens to tend and the eggs to gather. Not until she'd ducked down and entered the chicken coop did she vent the words that begged to escape earlier.

"Of all things! Handled carelessly and broken! Serves her right if she'd break one herself!" The chickens didn't seem to notice the girl's heartaches. They clucked and fussed as usual as they discussed among themselves where the best roosting spot might be.

The wire egg basket filled quickly with smooth, tawny eggs. Carefully Susannah added a third layer to the load. It would never do to break even one. This would bring at least a tongue lashing, if not a wallop of Mrs. Martin's hand.

Gingerly she transported the valuable eggs to the shanty. Her next job was to clean them and deposit them into crates.

Finally done, she headed to the house. Hearing thumps and shuffling in the kitchen, she assumed Mrs. Martin was preparing supper.

Not ready to face her yet, Susannah stepped through the doorway into the front room. Oh, there was Betsy's new dresser! And on top of it lay a large plate from the crate of new dishes. Breathlessly Susannah stepped closer. Oh, they were so lovely! All creamy white with a dainty strip of gold on the rim. And in the center was a cluster of pink blossoms.

Susannah hardly breathed. She'd never seen dishes more beautiful! No wonder Betsy had seemed to float on air when she'd come home from town. So enraptured was the girl in her observations that she didn't hear menacing steps come up behind her.

"I thought I told you to keep your hands off Betsy's dishes!" The shrill accusation came from right behind her.

"I haven't touched them!" Susannah exclaimed. Out of the corner of her eye she saw Mrs. Martin lift her arm as if to strike her. She ducked—but a trifle too late. With a sickening "Pop!" and a blast of pain, Mrs. Martin's fist slammed into her face. At first Susannah was too stunned to realize the sound had come from her own nose. She reached up to touch the hurting part of her face in shock. A strange lump met the tips of her fingers.

"My nose!" Susannah moaned. "You've broken my nose!" She stared wildly at her hand. Her fingers were covered with blood. That must be coming from her nose too.

A sob tore from her throat as she reached for the handkerchief in the pocket of her dress. But wiping her nose only brought on more pain.

In anguish Susannah's eyes met Mrs. Martin's. The expression of hate she saw there made her forget her pain for a few seconds. Wisdom beyond her years gave Susannah the thought that next came to her mind.

She's the one to be pitied, she concluded.

Shielding her face with her bloody hand, Susannah slid past the angry woman and out of the room.

chapter 6

Change in the Air

If Susannah thought her life difficult before, it became even more so after Betsy married and moved to Amos's farm. With Betsy no longer there to do any of the work, Susannah's chores multiplied. She also missed Betsy's companionship and the buffer she had furnished between her and the irritable Mrs. Martin.

No longer did Betsy's sweet soprano lift Susannah's spirits. Now she had to rely on her own memory for both the words and the singing. At first she disliked singing alone, but with time she realized that singing, even though alone, distracted her somewhat from her dismal situation.

She learned to do her work fast and well, even if no one took the time or kindness to compliment her for it. Now a teenager, she found satisfaction in seeing whether she could perform her ordinary tasks in such a way that no one could fault her.

This was certainly a challenge. Many times she received scoldings she didn't deserve. At a time in her life when young womanhood should have emerged freely and unaffectedly, Susannah subconsciously barred the door to her deepest feelings. It would never do to be seen with tears spilling from her dark eyes. She learned that the safest way was to bottle them up and save them until nightfall. Then, alone in her bedroom, they could flow unhindered.

There were also other things to occupy her young mind. One of these was changes in the church and in their way of living, the only things that had always been stable through her growing-up years.

As the Mennonite community in Ontario became better established, their prosperity brought about many subtle changes.

Indeed, all of North America was rapidly changing. With the advent of railroads into Ontario, merchandise from the larger United States cities became readily available. There was even talk of electricity making its way north into Ontario!

Susannah heard the talk of these topics swirl around her. Being a young woman made her especially aware of changes in the matter of clothing. The Mennonites had always maintained simple clothing, though they didn't have distinct dress codes to segregate them from other denominations. Now with textiles being produced on machinery, new styles were becoming readily available. The more progressive members soon began to borrow clothing patterns from their Protestant neighbors.

Betsy herself had begun to wear a strip of lace around the rim of her white head covering. Many of the other young women had added this adornment long before Betsy was allowed to.

How Susannah coveted that border on Betsy's covering! It was beautiful! But she knew better than to express a desire to have one herself. She well remembered how Mrs. Martin had scolded Betsy's extravagance. "Next thing you know Susannah's going to beg for lace too. And I'm not spending money on such nonsense for her!" She had sniffed loudly. "We have more important things to buy."

With that, the subject was closed. Susannah, having never stooped to beg for anything, didn't ask for lace. But the longing was strong to fit in with the other young women her age.

All these changes made some of the Canadian Mennonites uneasy. What was happening? Where would it lead? Would it lure them into a swirling vortex they might later wish they had no part of?

Some sided with the views of the Methodist movement that was sweeping across North America. That trend was to hold large revival meetings and place much emphasis on the emotional experience of being saved. They claimed the Mennonites held too strictly to traditions that were useless, rather than placing enough importance on spirituality.

A few families in Ontario still had contact with relatives in Pennsylvania. There, a group had withdrawn from the main Mennonite church because they believed the church was becoming too lax in church discipline and other matters. The leader of this offshoot was Jacob W. Stauffer. His following was dubbed the Stauffer Mennonites, or Old Order Mennonites.

It appeared that those Stauffer Mennonites, in spite of all their strict ways, were growing in number.

Talk flew thicker and faster than snowflakes in a winter blizzard. Some members of the Waterloo district wanted their bishop to organize an Old Order movement right here.

Bishop Abraham Martin was reluctant. He didn't relish the idea of leading a separation. He chose rather to try and hold neutral ground.

Some took this as an indication that their bishop was going to float along and allow all the changes and new ideas to become a part of their life. They wanted to begin a new, separate community where they could establish a lifestyle that kept them apart from the drift of worldly influences. But where should this settlement be? Should they move back to Pennsylvania where such a beginning had already been made?

That wouldn't be sensible. The high price of land there was part of the reason the first Mennonites had moved to Ontario to begin with.

Young Susannah realized that some families no longer attended the services at the meetinghouse on Sundays. The more conservative members had convinced a bishop from the Stauffer group in Pennsylvania to visit Ontario. These families now held their own services in homes of their members. It was to be a similar group to that of the Stauffer branch. Their goal was high. Based on Ephesians 5:27, it was to be "a glorious church, not having spot or wrinkle."

They soon ordained a bishop, Jesse Bauman, and a minister, Josiah

Martin. Still desiring to settle elsewhere, several members of the group made contact with a real estate agent who knew of unsettled land available in Iowa.

From all the talk she heard, Susannah knew that Iowa was a part of the United States, far away from Ontario. She knew she wasn't likely to ever see it, but she couldn't help but wonder what it looked like.

chapter 7

Iowa Community Begins

It was now the year 1888. A few families had left the year before and moved to that faraway prairie land of northwest Iowa. Their first year had been a lonely one. Letters were written home to Ontario encouraging others to join them.

Among others, the young minister Josiah Martin and his family now made plans to join them.

March winds whistled and tugged at anything that wasn't securely fastened. A large crowd milled about the Berlin train depot. Children, wrapped in layers of woolen garments, moved stiffly through the crowd. They were about to embark on the greatest journey of their lives.

All along the streets, hitching rails were lined up with teams hitched to wagons or sleds. Many belonged to families or neighbors who had brought in the departing families for the beginning of their move.

A casual onlooker wouldn't have known which people were the ones actually moving away and which were merely well-wishers. Those moving had already loaded their possessions on empty freight cars. Their livestock would go in a stock car. And for the nearly fifty people leaving, there was a reserved passenger car.

The open fields surrounding Berlin did nothing to stop the wind whooshing across the snow. The crowd shivered, but was it actually from the cold, or was it from the excitement that filled the air and their minds? As people bade farewell to each other, they were fully aware that they might never see each other again.

Finally, with much huffing and steaming, the great iron train pulled away from the station. An emptiness settled over the depot. Wagons and sleds were driven home to a community which now also seemed much emptier.

Seven families left Ontario that day. Susannah didn't actually know any of these people very well, as her life at the Martins didn't allow her many social contacts.

Gradually letters from the new settlement in Iowa drifted back to Ontario. They didn't bring good news.

The Martins discussed these tidings around their supper table a few months later.

"When they got to Iowa, the snow was still so deep they couldn't get any work done," Mr. Martin informed them. "They couldn't get started working on their buildings right away as they had planned."

"What did they do?" Christy asked.

Susannah was all ears. She knew better than to ask any questions, but she certainly wondered how those families had fared.

"They moved in with the few who moved there last year. Some of them lived in granaries and slept in barns because their houses wouldn't hold them all."

"Oh, my." This even aroused Mrs. Martin's sympathies.

"Ya, then in April, when they were barely there a month, the measles hit." Mr. Martin paused to swallow a bite. "Four families each lost a child to the measles in less than a month's time."

Even the work-hardened faces of Reuben and Elias registered an expression of pain at this.

"They had to start a cemetery and dig graves for those children before they even got started on a home to live in." There was a catch in Mr. Martin's voice as he said this.

"Why didn't they get a doctor?" asked Christy.

"It's too far away for a doctor to come in the winter," Mr. Martin replied. "But they wanted that. They believed the farther away from town and its influences they live, the less struggle they'll have with worldly things. Besides, measles aren't something a doctor can cure."

The last fact rang with a chill of truth. Death was never far away from anyone. Measles, diphtheria, typhoid, and pneumonia were all deadly. They could strike any household, and did so, with no respect of persons. Even doctors could only do so much. The hand of God could heal or claim lives however He saw fit. This knowledge was a part of life.

chapter 8

Ontario Turmoil

S truggles in the Ontario group weren't over just because some of the more conservative ones had moved to Iowa.

New things such as Sunday School, revival meetings, and the use of the English language were making inroads into the community. Clothing styles were becoming increasingly modern. By now it was clear that if no limits were placed on these practices, they would indeed lose out on many of the important convictions of their forefathers.

In 1889 Bishop Martin concluded that a tighter rein needed to be kept on the congregation. He and his followers separated from the established Mennonites in Ontario and also formed an Old Order group. They decided that a plain, distinctive dress needed to separate Christians from the worldly society, and set out to outline what that meant for the congregation. They took seriously the command of II Cor. 6:17-18, "Wherefore come out from among them, and be ye separate, saith the Lord, and touch not the unclean thing; and I will receive you, and will be a Father unto you, and ye shall be my sons and daughters, saith the Lord Almighty."

Opposition from the main branch was strong. Ample expression of one's faith was all that was necessary, they said, not excessive rules to distract one.

The test of time would be the only means of showing which group actually maintained the principles of a Christian life. Verbally, the opposition claimed to have their faith just as firmly intact. With much ridicule directed their way, the cautious Old Order group chose to keep the door of modernity closed to their congregation.

Conversations on all these topics swirled around Susannah throughout her teen years. For the most part, these issues had little actual impact on her life. Adults had always made the choices in her life. Her part was to obey the decisions—or suffer the consequences.

When the Martin family chose to become part of the Old Order group, it didn't bring about any immediate changes in her life. Even if other young women her age had allowed themselves some finery, Susannah had continued to wear her plain clothes.

All these distractions and talk kept life lively for Susannah. Focusing on all the shifting scenes kept her from dwelling dismally on the things that did not change for the better in her own life.

On top of all this, Betsy and Amos were parents now. A son, Anson, had joined their home in 1888. He was soon followed by a sister, Mary, in 1890.

Though Susannah had nieces and nephews in her own siblings' families, these children of Betsy's were the ones she had the most contact with.

In the fall of 1890 Susannah received news that sister Franey and her husband George had twins! According to word of mouth, they were named Edgar and Mary Edna.

Susannah's brother Moses was married to Amanda Otterbein. They too received a tiny daughter that summer. Sister Mary Ann was getting ready to marry as well.

With the passing of seasons, time marched on and brought about changes in the family and on the farm.

Then, with the dark skies of winter of 1895, came a dreaded word that sent chills up and down everyone's back—diphtheria.

chapter 9

Diphtheria

Susannah heard of it at the meetinghouse on Sunday. This was the only time she met any of her own family. Sometimes there was time for a brief visit with Mother after the services were over, before the Martins left for home.

"Did you know George and Franey are under quarantine?" was Mother's question that day.

"No," Susannah answered. "Why?"

"The children have gotten diphtheria." This needed no more explanation. The name of the dreaded sickness was enough to strike terror in any heart. "It sounds as though the twins have it worst."

"Oh, my!" Susannah knew that small children were the most vulnerable targets for the awful sickness.

Mother and daughter faced each other wordlessly. There seemed little to say.

At that moment Mrs. Martin called across the pew to Susannah. "Come. We're starting home."

Susannah followed, her heart heavy with dread.

The next week brought heavy snow from the north. Day was nearly as dark as night. The wind howled and shrieked around the buildings of the farm. Wind-driven snow hurled itself against anything in its path. Deep drifts formed in the fields and pastures.

All but the most necessary work ceased. The Martin men burned all their energy in extra efforts to merely get the ordinary chores done. Mrs. Martin and Susannah were trapped in the kitchen most days, which was the only heated room in the house. It took nearly constant vigilance to keep the fire blazing in defiance to the brutal storm outdoors.

Susannah's mind often wandered in the direction of her older sister's home. How were the sick little ones faring?

There was no way to find out. The quarantine alone forbade any visitors to the home. And no one could have safely made the trip through the raging wind and blinding snow anyway.

There was nothing to do but wait. And pray. Susannah found her thoughts rising above the storm to the God who controlled it. She didn't understand how He could hear her small, silent pleas for intervention.

As long as she could remember, she had attended the services at the meetinghouse on Sundays. Now that she was older, she began to believe for herself the truths the ministers expounded from the black German Bible each Sunday. Much about God was a mystery to her, but she did understand the need for a habit of prayer. She now turned to the Lord with pleadings for healing of those sick little ones. After all, if anyone could help them, it was God.

Days later the storm finally whirled its way out of the community. Having spent its fury, it slunk away with a parting breath of icy air. Deep and impassable drifts crippled any hope of travel throughout the neighborhood. The sun finally emerged, but it was no match for the frigid winds.

Finally word spread Susannah's way that the crisis had passed in Franey's home. But not in the way humans had hoped.

One of the twins, four-year-old Mary Edna, had been claimed by death. Edgar was no longer part of a pair, for his playmate had been taken from his side.

Susannah's heart was heavy with a feeling of loss for this niece who she hadn't really had the opportunity to know.

Because of the quarantine still in effect, along with the deep snowdrifts, plans were to observe a funeral service at a later date.

Why does God let things like this happen? Susannah wondered. From what she understood, it would seem as if He could prevent sickness and death. If He was all-powerful and all-knowing, then why didn't He perform a miracle like He did many times in the Bible? Questions swirled through Susannah's mind. How she wished for a talk with Betsy! Nearly always Betsy could answer her disturbing questions.

And if she couldn't, she patiently explained to the younger girl that God's ways were beyond finding out. No one understood His plans perfectly. No one on earth, anyway. There were a lot of things one might never understand as long as one lived. And for those things, it is best to trust Him, and believe that He has a plan.

A deep sigh escaped Susannah as she mulled over these things. Right now it wasn't possible to talk with Betsy, and she wasn't comfortable airing her jumbled thoughts to anyone else here at the Martins.

Many days later, after the child's funeral service was finally held, Susannah learned something that puzzled her still more. It seemed that now, after having passed through the ordeal of burying their small daughter, George and Franey had decided to become baptized and yield their lives to the Lord.

Susannah understood that this step was important. Baptism, according to what she had gathered at church, was to be an outward ceremony that proved a change had taken place in one's heart. It meant that one had decided to trust and believe in the God who had sent His only Son to the cross to purify humans' sinful hearts. It meant that you were willing to live a humble life as free from sin as humanly possible. It included a solemn promise to remain faithful as long as one lived. It also meant that when one died, God had promised to receive all such believers into His heavenly kingdom.

Susannah wondered how her sister could trust God after this trial of sickness and death? What mysterious force caused her to now place her belief in a Creator and Lord whom one could never fully understand?

For a long time the young woman pondered these things. She became aware of a strong longing in her own heart. A yearning to lay aside these troubling doubts and simply trust the great God of heaven.

chapter 10

New Faith and Large Fears

Susannah's assignment for today was to work the spinning wheel. Nearly every farmer kept a few sheep to provide wool for warm winter clothes. Now that woolen mills dotted the countryside and fabric was made there on large weaving machines, each family kept only enough sheep for wool to make their own stockings, warm winter slippers, scarves, and mittens.

Wool shearing took place in early summer. This was preceded by driving the sheep to the creek nearby and administering a bath which the sheep reluctantly received. They were then left to dry a few days before the shearing took place.

Shorn wool which came off in one big piece was then sorted into grades. The cleanest, softest wool, from the shoulders and back, was for making the best grade of clothing. Wool from the other parts of the sheep was dirtier and coarser, so it was set aside for unrefined use.

Susannah was relieved when the tedious chore of carding was past. She sighed, remembering the long hours spent with the hand carder. Wool had to be cleaned of dirt, and the many teeth on the handheld carder served to remove debris stuck in the curly fibers. One had to do it over and over. Afterwards, the fibers were strung into a long strand of slightly twisted wool called a roving.

Susannah took the steps two at a time up to the attic. Her eyes adjusted slowly to the dimness. Gathering up a large armful of the ticklish, soft rovings they'd stored there, she returned to the front room. One more trip to the attic to fetch the spinning wheel, and she would be nearly ready.

Carefully she placed the spinning wheel upon the floor, scooting it around to a level spot, so the four-legged frame wouldn't wobble.

Swiping a layer of attic dust from the treadle and blowing a quick puff to dislodge a coating that had settled on the whirl, she finally took her seat on the low stool next to the spinning wheel.

Grabbing the empty wooden spindle, she settled it into place. Gently she placed her right foot upon the treadle and pushed. Obediently the wheel spun, but not without a protesting squeak.

This won't do. Susannah rose to fetch the can of tallow kept behind the stove. Gathering a generous lump on the tip of her forefinger she smeared it onto the wooden part from which the squeak had come. She turned the wheel with her left hand. Now it revolved silently.

Susannah chuckled to herself. *No wonder the saying goes that the squeaky wheel gets the grease!* Settling again, she gathered an end of the roving and twisted it between her fingers. She bent her head to peer into the tiny hole through which she'd need to thread the roving. Getting started was sometimes a trick, but today it went smoothly and Susannah was pleased.

She straightened and pushed her foot upon the treadle again. Then, gathering the roving, she began to spin. It was ticklish business to feed it at just the right tension into the small hole. If she held it too loosely, the spun strand would be weak and tear off.

Getting started required all of Susannah's attention. One must pedal the treadle just so. The wheel must not be allowed to spin backwards, or the spun strand would unravel from the spindle. At the same time, she must hold the roving just right. If she held it too tightly, it would spin a strand so tightly that it twisted back upon itself in an ugly snarl.

Today it was just a matter of getting off to a good start. But Susannah recalled the difficult time she'd experienced while learning this chore years ago. Even now, echoes of impatient scoldings bounced around in her memory. The more she was ridiculed, the tenser she became. The result was a very unhappy girl who sat under these lessons. The crowning insult was always to be compared to Betsy, who could spin very efficiently. Even now the memory of those taunts caused an almost bitter flavor in Susannah's mouth.

A steady up and down press of her foot kept the wheel spinning smoothly. Her hands were both occupied at the task of feeding the roving into the device which drew it hungrily and at the same time twisted it into a strand of yarn and wound it neatly onto the spindle.

Susannah's thoughts whirled as she spun. Now that she was off to a good start, her mind had liberty to roam over the events of late.

The most important was the baptism she'd received lately. The heavy weight of indecision had pressed upon her, nagging her thoughts until she was miserable. She had finally been sure that it was what she believed, and that she wished it to be done and then over with. It was the nerve-wracking process of making her desire known to the bishop, and then the congregation, that caused her dread.

A huge part of her struggle had been to have the Martins find out of her convictions. Though they remained faithful to the new Old Order Mennonite group led by Bishop Abraham Martin, it wasn't a household of shining examples otherwise. Much of Susannah's struggle with her conscience was a battle of wanting to accept her Lord Jesus as Lord and Saviour of her life. The other half of her shrank from the reality of her daily trials. How could she live out her newfound convictions in this environment of bitterness and hostility? She had only to reach up to feel the hump on the bridge of her nose as a reminder that beatings were common here. Why it was so, she had not yet understood. There was no one to confide in.

She knew from the depths of her heart that she didn't wish to ever become like that herself. This caused her no small amount of turmoil. How could she respond meekly when treated wrongly? Many times the ugly anger of injustice boiled within her. Would it ever become easier to respond mildly to the stormy atmosphere of her daily life? Would she ever be able to do anything right? Where else could she go? Not just anyone took in the unwanted Heckendorn clan.

Her thoughts spun nearly as fast as the wooden spindle revolved. She recalled the day following her baptism when she had received her first Holy Communion. As he dealt out the sacraments of dark wine and crusty bread to the members of the congregation, Bishop Abraham had expounded on the treatment Christ had received from His own people. He, the Son of God who had come to save the world, had been rejected. Mocked. Whipped. Spit upon. At last He was hung on a crude cross in public humiliation and awful pain. And what had been His response?

Susannah could still hear the bishop repeating Jesus' words in a husky voice. "Oh, Father, forgive them, for they know not what they do!" Even now she recalled the tingle of wine as it warmed her throat. It had seemed to warm even her heart. Later she was aware that her heart remained warm, not merely because of the wine, but from her deep desire to respond like that to her situation.

Could she do it? With each ounce of her being, that was her desire. Now in the days and weeks that followed, she was finding out that it was as hard as she'd feared.

Though now that she was an adult the beatings weren't physical, there was still the scalding tirade of ridicule. At least on Mrs. Martin's part.

Susannah paused to lift out the full spindle and place it in the crate beside her. Swiftly she replaced it with an empty one and resumed spinning.

The change that worried her most was Mr. Martin's behavior. Susannah couldn't recall when his conduct had changed. She only knew she wished for the safe return of only his angry eyes and scoldings.

Now when he watched her his eyes held a sickening possessive expression. It made her want to disappear. It made her feel ugly and soiled in a way she couldn't describe. It made her determined to avoid him if she could possibly do so.

Even now, at only the thought of it, her heart beat faster with fear. For he could not always be avoided...

chapter 11

Divine Deliverance

It was June of 1896. Susannah's twenty-first birthday would be this week. She knew that other people began to earn their own wages then. In fact, she knew of people who'd been paid their own money before then. But what of her? Would this milestone make any difference for her?

She did know that she wished to leave the Martins. If only she could get up the courage to do it! But where could she go? Who would want her? She owned absolutely nothing. That meant she'd likely have to start out working in another household. But who knew if it would be any different there?

Well, it can't be much worse, can it? she asked herself grimly one morning as she milked the cow before breakfast. She leaned her dark head against the warm flank of the cow. Her small, strong hands expertly sent frothy white streams into the foamy bucket at her feet.

"Lord," she pleaded. "Please help something to change, if it is your will. You see how it is here. You know I have reason to fear. What shall I do? Where can I go? Please show me, and guide me somehow." She paused after this petition.

Then, in a moment of total submission to her Lord, she added a final plea, "Or show me how to bear it if I must."

She switched to the other side of the cow, gently moving the bucket into position. This time of morning solitude suited her well. No one had ever bothered her here. Before the other orders of the day came, this predictable chore soothed her spirit. But it didn't last long enough. Soon the milk in her bucket neared the top, and it was time to return to the house and face whatever she must.

The beauty of the early summer morning was lost on her as she headed toward the house. Even the cheerful warble of a bluebird in the maple tree was lost on her.

Entering the kitchen door with the milk pail, she glanced cautiously at Mrs. Martin. The woman glared at her, with lips set in a thin, straight line.

Susannah lifted the heavy bucket and set it carefully on the wooden dry sink.

"Don't set that pail up there! It's all dirty from the barn! Don't you know better?" The sharp words rained on her.

The handle, still in Susannah's hand, was lifted again. She looked bewilderedly around the kitchen for another safe place to set it. The pail was no dirtier than before. Only yesterday she'd been scolded for setting the bucket on the floor, which she'd always done before.

"Set it by the door there," came the order now. "On the floor. Get on with your breakfast. The dishes are waiting on you."

Though she had little appetite after this exchange, Susannah filled a bowl of oatmeal for herself from the pot on the back of the stove. Numbly she sat at the table amidst the family's dishes still remaining there. She would need the strength of this food to face the rest of today.

She was relieved to hear the bedroom door slam shut behind Mrs. Martin as she left the kitchen. Maybe she was to be left in peace to eat this food.

Peace. It seemed an impossible quest to Susannah. She didn't wonder that Mrs. Martin despised her more than ever lately. The woman wasn't blind. She could not have missed her husband's attempts at improper contact with Susannah. Nor could she have missed the fact that the young woman was repulsed by his actions. So much so that she went to great lengths to avoid him altogether. All of it created a strained awkwardness for Mrs. Martin. Never a happy person, she now directed this added bitterness toward Susannah.

The resulting strain upon Susannah was consuming her plucky spirit more each day that passed.

If only there were someone she could talk to! This futile wish produced a salty tear that slipped down her cheek and plopped into her bowl of oatmeal. Who would understand this depraved situation, should she ever get up the nerve to speak of it? Would anyone believe her? Would it change anything? Oh, and this was only Monday morning! The bleakness of another week stretched out before Susannah's distressed mind. How was she to bear it? Would there ever be an end to this terrible situation?

She rose after having swallowed the last spoonful of her tasteless oatmeal. Automatically she cleared the table of the soiled dishes left behind by the men in the family. Stacking them numbly, she fetched the steaming teakettle and prepared water to wash them.

Absently she heard a team and wagon rattle into the barnyard. Normally out of curiosity she'd glance out the window to see if someone had come, or if it was only one of the menfolk going about their work. This morning it mattered little to her darkened spirit who it might be.

Presently a hearty knock pounded upon the front door. Mrs. Martin came from the bedroom and went to answer it.

"Good morning." Susannah recognized the voice of Amos, Betsy's husband, at the door.

"Good morning," his mother-in-law returned.

Hearing her voice, Susannah marveled at the change in tone from when it was directed at herself.

"Come on in. What brings you this morning?" Mrs. Martin inquired in her Sunday voice.

"Well, you know, Betsy isn't doing so well. She hasn't found a maid yet for the summer. She's gotten the idea that she'd like to have Susannah to help her out. She thought maybe you could spare her." Amos stated his mission and waited.

Susannah couldn't believe her ears. She waited, as stunned by the request as Mrs. Martin must be, as long as it was taking her to reply. Barely breathing, Susannah waited for Mrs. Martin to declare her fate. She dared not hope. But then the thought popped into her head that surely God had responded to her nearly frantic plea for deliverance.

Never having developed the habit of denying her only daughter's requests, Susannah heard Mrs. Martin slowly answer Amos.

"I just don't know..." The words hung. Then in a more decided tone, she said, "You say Betsy isn't doing so well? Then I guess Susannah must go help her."

"I'd take her along now," Amos stated. "Is she close by? Can she get ready?"

Mrs. Martin now came into the kitchen, where Susannah stood motionless.

"Finish the dishes. Then get your clothes and go with Amos." The curt order held no emotion. "You will stay there." These last four words nearly sounded triumphant to Susannah. Fleetingly the thought flew through Susannah's mind that perhaps the woman was as glad to see her leave as she was to go.

Later Susannah couldn't recall having done the rest of the morning dishes. Nor of collecting her only other dress. Bewilderment still possessed her at this sudden turn of events. She hadn't assumed deliverance would come this suddenly or this simply! It boggled her mind, the joy of it!

She followed Amos to the wagon and at his bidding climbed to the high seat.

Briskly Amos untied the horse and hopped on board. Reining the team away from the hitching post, he guided them out the lane.

Beyond the sides of her bonnet, from the corner of her eye, Susannah caught a glimpse of a figure by the barn door. It was Mr. Martin, staring after the team in surprise. Amos lifted his hand as they passed. Susannah looked away quickly. An involuntary shudder shook her petite frame.

"Thank you, Lord, for answering my prayers," she breathed silently. The gratitude came from the depths of her heart.

chapter 12

Safety

Amos and Betsy's farm was located not far from the tiny hamlet of Wallenstein. Susannah found comfort in the fact that it was a fair distance north of the Martin household. There was little chance of meeting them suddenly and causing her fears to rebound.

Betsy was now the busy mother of five children. Little Christina wasn't yet a year old. There was no lack of work on a farm in summer, either for the men, who did the farming, or the women, who took care of the home and children. The women's work included growing and preparing food to place upon the table daily, and also to preserve food for the long winter months.

Anson, at eight, spent most of his time helping his father in the fields. There was plenty for a little man his size to do. Mary, Lydia, Magdalena, and the baby weren't big enough to be much help, but were underfoot in their attempts.

Susannah, not accustomed to a household with small children, found the change a pleasant distraction. Their chatter and countless questions amused her. It also kept her mind from turning back to the complicated tangle of worries she'd left behind.

Betsy was the only friend Susannah had ever known. It was a balm to her harassed mind to be under the same roof again. Now, however, Betsy's time was taken up with her own family. There was scant time for any long talks. That suited Susannah. She couldn't have made herself tell of the trials she'd suffered at the hand of Betsy's parents. Besides, Betsy knew how it had been before she'd married and left home. That nothing had improved since then was a detail Susannah didn't wish to reveal. The shame was too great. The feeling of ugliness that came with it was one Susannah wished to bury forever.

Here at last, by a miraculous deliverance of the God in whom Susannah was learning to trust, she felt free and safe. This last reason released the weight that had so long pressed upon Susannah's slight shoulders.

She dug into the work each day with delight. It was spring after all. The time when happy birds didn't cease singing from sunrise until they whispered their vespery warbles to each other at the close of day.

Fresh garden earth awaited the tiny dark seeds that were buried at seedtime. Rich, brown, and crumbly, the earth closed over those small promises of food to come forth in the sunny days ahead. Gentle rains from the skies above moistened a breath of new life into them. The orchard was clothed in frilly garments of fairest white and dainty pink.

Tall maples sported new, soft green leaves. They had donated their annual late winter lifeblood of sap to the family. It had been laboriously collected and cooked at the sugar camp. Jugs of amber syrup lined the cellar floor. Barrels were filled with a fresh supply of crusty brown sugar, sweet enough to please even the most winter-dulled tongues.

Susannah's twenty-first birthday passed with no ado. Betsy made no mention of it. Therefore, Susannah was very surprised when Betsy opened the subject late on Saturday afternoon

"Well, Susannah," Betsy began offhandedly, "we won't be able to pay you much, but I sure do appreciate your help. Would you rather be paid now, or should I use the money to buy you some goods for a new dress for summer?"

Susannah stared at Betsy in bewilderment. Such matters had never been left to her choosing before. Didn't Betsy know that?

"What do you think best?" she finally asked.

"Your dress is worn out," Betsy said bluntly. "I believe I'll get you that first. What else do you need?"

"I don't know. Nothing, for now," Susannah answered.

"You can get the dress made as soon as we get the material. We'll go from there. If you decide you'd rather have the wages after that, it's up to you."

"How much will the goods cost?" Susannah wondered. This new world of buying her own clothes with her own money was as strange to her as if the sheep had suddenly begun to grow feathers instead of wool.

"The last I bought was nearly eight cents a yard," Betsy said. "It just keeps going up."

"Oh!" Susannah exclaimed. "I'll have to work a while to earn that back."

That night when Susannah went upstairs to the small bedroom she shared with the little girls, she had plenty to occupy her thoughts.

It was all so new and strange. Exciting even. But also a bit scary in its newness. How was she to handle it all? She would have to ask for Betsy's help, no doubt.

Before she had finished that thought, another one hit her. She knelt beside the bed to ask for divine help as well.

"Dear Lord," she whispered. "Thank you for all this. Thank you for sending me to Betsy's home. Of all places, there's nowhere else I'd rather be. Please show me how to earn my keep and to use the money as you see fit."

There was more. By the time Susannah slipped between the bed linens she felt calm and peaceful. It was such an unusual feeling for her that she soon fell asleep.

In the following days Betsy was as good as her word. The next time she and Amos went to Hawksville with the team for supplies, she brought home a length of navy dress fabric for Susannah. She also saw to it that there was time to cut it carefully. In the evenings after dishes were done, Susannah was free to do the sewing.

When it was finished at last, Susannah surveyed it with a grateful heart. The fact that she'd earned it herself made her extra careful when she carried it upstairs to hang from the nail on the bedroom wall.

"Will you wear it to the meetinghouse on Sunday?" asked young Mary.

"Yes. It will be only for Sundays," Susannah answered. "I'll wear my other one on weekdays."

"And the one you have on now can go on the rug pile, can't it?" Mary had been taught well by her thrifty mother.

"Yes. It's so worn out, it's barely fit for that," Susannah said.

"Mine don't go to the rug pile," Mary informed her. "Lydia gets them when they don't fit me anymore."

"Mary is the only one who gets new dresses," Lydia said soberly. "We get her old ones."

Susannah knew the feeling well. "I always wore the ones your mother outgrew too," she told the young lass.

"Were you her sister?" Lydia asked, surveying Susannah with wide eyes.

"No, but I lived with her." Susannah kept the details simple.

"And now you live with us!" Mary stated happily.

"And you have a new dress!" Lydia added.

"Yes!" Susannah agreed to both. "I'm very happy to be here too!"

"Are you happy about the dress?" Lydia persisted.

"Oh, yes! I am!" Susannah smiled down at both of them. *If you girls only knew how happy I am to be here!* she thought silently. Then aloud she suggested, "Come, we should go back downstairs and get to work."

chapter 13

An Adult Pupil

Summer flew by swiftly, with scarcely any dull moments. Work which otherwise might have been tedious and repetitive was kept lively with the children's attempts at helping. Their willing spirits and busy little hands could help quite a bit if they were directed in the right way.

There were huge dinners to prepare for the extra men Amos hired at haying time, and then again at harvest time.

Autumn brought a bounty of juicy apples from the trees which had sported such clouds of blossoms in the spring. Susannah snitzed apples by the pailful. These were dried for winter use. Barrels were packed away into the cellar to be eaten raw well into the winter.

There was corn to husk, most of which was fed to the animals during the winter. Betsy sorted out what her family would likely use. This was roasted and ground into cornmeal. The biggest, fattest cobs were selected to store in the attic for next year's seed.

Bunches of sage were gathered to hang upside down from the attic rafters. This was to be used for seasoning the sausages at butchering time. It was also used as a hot tea to drink at the first hint of a sore throat.

When the first snows blew upon the household, Betsy and Susannah were confident that they had prepared for the season as well as they could.

Now it was time to get out the spinning wheel, the knitting needles, and rags for rug making. Susannah soon learned that Betsy had other plans too.

"Mary is old enough to start learning the alphabet this winter," Betsy declared. "She might as well start now while I have free time from all the outdoor work."

"Yes! Yes!" Mary cheered. "I want to learn to read!"

"I want to read too!" Lydia chimed in. "May I?"

"No. You'll learn when you're older," Betsy told her. "You can be a big help if you play nicely with Magdalena and Christina. Then maybe Susannah can study too." This last sounded like an off-hand suggestion.

"Can't you read, Susannah?" Mary was incredulous.

Susannah felt her face flush. "Not very well," she admitted.

"Do you want to?" came the next question.

"Yes," Susannah said wistfully. "I always wanted to go to school."

Again Betsy was as good as her word. She ran her household efficiently. A few hours each day were soon set aside for lessons.

Susannah couldn't believe how fast young Mary caught on. As for herself, there was precious little she had retained from her early, meager classroom hours.

"Ach," she complained to Betsy one day. "Maybe it's a waste of time for me to study books. What good will it do me now? I got along without it for so long."

"Everyone needs to learn to read," Betsy insisted. "You surely want to read the Bible, don't you?"

Susannah nodded.

"And read hymns. I know how you enjoy singing," Betsy added.

"Oh, yes!" Susannah agreed. "I guess there's more value in learning to read than I thought."

Ontario winters had never been mild, and this one was no exception. Hoarfrost grew thick and white in the cold temperatures. Then the landscape was covered in blankets of snow. Icicles grew long and pointed along the edge of the eaves. Howl and shriek as it might, the wind couldn't distract the two students in the kitchen that winter.

One was a fresh young mind of seven years. The other, a determined, slight young woman of nearly twenty two. The first one soaked up new information like a dry sponge might soak up spilled milk. The other, whose mind and heart already knew so many things that weren't taught from books, had to work much harder.

Betsy taught her pupils well. Before long, what had at first seemed like meaningless scribbles on the slate became familiar shapes. After much practice, these shapes could be strung together to form words. Then into sentences.

Once the allotted time of study had passed for the day, Susannah found that she could practice mentally while she did her other work. Sewing, knitting, spinning, and even cooking and baking could be turned into scholarly exercises. Of course, she was careful not to neglect the work while her mind was mulling over the shapes and sounds of the alphabet.

By the time the baby arrived to join Amos and Betsy's family, Mary and Susannah were far enough along to continue some of the studies on their own.

The little one was named Lizzie. Betsy's four other daughters' joy knew no bounds at the arrival of this sister.

Anson wondered if it wasn't about time for another boy instead of so many little sisters.

"Ach, no," Amos teased him. "With all these girls, you and I won't have to worry about washing dishes."

Before long, Betsy was back out in her kitchen. The rocking chair by the stove became her seat of honor with the new baby. From here she could direct the studies once again.

And she could also sing. Patiently she explained to Susannah the meaning of the tiny symbols that framed the words in the songbook. They were called "notes," and like the alphabet letters, each one had its own sound.

Thirstily Susannah absorbed all this information. The more she learned about singing, the more poetic the words of the hymns became. The deep meaning of the words often spoke to her heart and soul. Sometimes Betsy sang the slower-paced German songs sung at church. These were the easiest ones, for the language was both her and Susannah's first language. Susannah marveled time and again that words written so long ago by unknown people could still today so closely mimic what was in her own heart.

From her time among the young folks, Betsy also learned many English hymns. Though some of these words were harder to read, Susannah loved to sing them too. Day after day the two women sang as they worked. Had the passing winds paused to listen, they would have noticed the sweet music filling the humble house. They might even have envied the soft notes rising and falling, carrying the lovely words of prayer and praise upward through the roof and into the skies—ascending to their Maker's throne.

Susannah wasn't aware that this memorizing of songs and melodies was being stored deep within her memory chest. She had no way of knowing that she was building an account from which she could withdraw deeply in years to come.

chapter 14

Betsy Insists

Susannah found life at Amos and Betsy's home very comfortable. For this reason she was upset at first when Betsy expressed another idea for change.

"Susannah," Betsy said one day. "I think you need to get out among the young folks. You should have friends your own age."

"What will you think of next?" Susannah gasped. "You are all the friend I need."

Betsy smiled at her. "I'm not your age, really. And I'm all tied down with my family. I know how I enjoyed my time with the young people. I want you to have a good time too."

"Ach," Susannah muttered. "I don't think I'd fit in. I'm just..." she lowered her breath. "A nobody," she finished.

"Now, now," Betsy chided. "You're as good as anyone else. We could make you another dress for outings. And I have some lace that would look good on the edge of your coverings. For your good ones, at least."

Susannah balked inwardly. She knew, though, that once Betsy had an idea there was no stopping her. So she said no more, but she thought plenty. Even with another new dress, and all the lace-edged coverings in Canada, she would still feel clumsy. Clumsy, and what was that other feeling? She guessed it was the old unwanted and ugly things that haunted her. Now they all rose to the surface again, taunting her. Not even an entire new wardrobe could change all that. She would still be the same old Susannah Heckendorn.

On Sundays at the meetinghouse she sometimes chatted with some of the girls who were part of the youth group. Though they were friendly enough, Susannah always felt at the edge of things. Hearing their talk of activities, and not being included made her feel like the crust in a loaf of bread. Most of the girls were younger than she was. They were also better dressed by far. And yes, lace on their coverings was a normal detail. In her younger years Susannah had coveted that strip of finery, but ever since Betsy's mother had predicted she'd be begging for that unnecessary frill she had not breathed a word of that desire. Now here was Betsy offering it! The years had taught Susannah that it wasn't the finery of the clothes a person wore, but the contents of the heart that really mattered. Even with clothes comparable to what the others had, Susannah was sure she'd still feel awkward. The other girls acted so graceful, so confident, so happy and carefree. Ach! Betsy didn't know what she was asking of her! She would never fit in with the young folks!

"You've saved a bit of money," Betsy continued, ignorant of the turmoil in Susannah's breast. "We can use that to get the goods for a dress. And a coat! You'll need a nice coat! I know just the kind to get for you."

Susannah stared at her. Betsy with a plan was like a team of horses running too fast. She needed someone to provide a safety brake! Susannah attempted it now.

"What if I spend all my money, then need it for something else?" she asked.

"What else do you need?" Betsy asked pleasantly.

"Nothing, really," Susannah admitted.

"Let's see. Next time we go for supplies, we'll get the things for you. I'll make a list," Betsy went on.

Seeing it was no use, Susannah resigned herself. At least it would be a few weeks or a month before they would get to town. In the meantime she could get used to the idea. And then it would take time to get a dress made. The comfort of knowing that this new turn of events wouldn't be upon her tomorrow was a relief.

In the coming days, Susannah's mind busily explored the possibilities that lay ahead for her. Surprisingly, as she got used to Betsy's idea, she rather liked it. In fact, she found herself almost looking forward to it.

On the day of the next trip to town, she found herself nearly as excited as the little girls as they awaited the returning team's clip-clops as they pulled the wagon into the barnyard. The girls knew their parents nearly always brought some small treat home for them. Susannah felt silly. Half of her couldn't wait to see what Betsy had purchased for her. The other half chided her childish anticipation.

Last week she and Betsy had carefully counted out the sum Susannah had saved. Betsy wasn't frivolous, even if she was full of ideas. Out loud she figured what the fabric might cost. She counted that off from the rest of Susannah's money. Then she calculated what a new coat might run. Carefully she counted the rest. Susannah hardly dared breathe. Would it be enough? Or would she be in debt for something that wasn't even her idea?

Never in her life had she had a new coat. She was barely getting used to having a new dress. What would it be like to wear a brand-new coat not worn thin in spots, with not a single patch anywhere?

"I think I hear them!" Mary exclaimed, interrupting Susannah's thoughts.

"I do too!" Lydia agreed.

The two little girls bounced up and down, their eyes shining with anticipation. Sure enough, Amos's team of bays pulling the wagon rounded the curve and trotted smartly up to the barn.

Susannah busied herself with some trivial kitchen detail. Betsy's daughters knew no such reserve. Making a dash out the door they met their parents nearly before the team stopped.

Seconds later they came dashing back, squealing excitedly. Mary, leading the pack, clutched in her hand a brown paper bag containing their treat for today.

"Look, Susannah!" Lydia beat her with the announcement. "Mother and Father brought us candy! It's pink!"

By now Betsy, laden with bundles, came in the door. Swishing her shawl, she unloaded parcels on the kitchen table. "Now, girls," she remonstrated. "These are Susannah's things. Don't touch them with your sticky fingers."

"Come, Susannah," she beckoned. "I think you'll be pleased."

Susannah wiped her hands on her apron. Carefully she cut the string around the largest bundle. Opening it up, she found a coat that took her breath away. Her hands trembled as she held it up. It was wool. Black and soft. It would be the warmest coat Susannah ever had. Her eyes took in the style of it. Betsy had chosen well. It was exactly like the other Mennonite women here wore. Susannah opened the front and felt the lining. Oh, it was unbelievable! Finally she dared meet Betsy's eyes.

"Was there…did you have enough money?" she asked voicing her fear.

"Yes, there was a little left over, Betsy assured her, her eyes twinkling merrily. "But knowing you, you'll work extra hard anyway! Now look at the fabric for the dress."

Susannah felt overwhelmed already, but she laid aside the coat and picked up the next bundle at Betsy's gesture.

Inside was a length of fabric. It was woolen too, of a dress weight. The solid color was as deep green as pine needles. Susannah fingered it silently. Her mind flew in all directions. Such finery! Why, she didn't deserve any of it! She was, after all, only Susannah Heckendorn—one of those children who had to be supported by others. How was it possible that she now had brand-new clothes, as nice as anyone else ever had? And they were paid for with her own money, not someone else's charity.

No matter how she might try, Susannah found it impossible to express how much this meant to her. So she simply said, "Oh, Betsy! Thank you so much!" Then she turned away quickly so the children wouldn't see the tears that threatened to spill down her cheeks.

chapter 15

A Knitting Party

The new dress was cut and sewn. It was made in the simple, long-sleeved style worn by the Mennonite women in Waterloo. The cape was ample and pointed. There were no frills. Even so, Susannah felt unworthy of it. She was glad the lace Betsy had produced to attach to the edge of her white covering was of the narrow kind. She wouldn't have liked the wider, frillier type the younger girls wore. With tiny, straight stitches she fastened it. Why, it looked…just right, she decided. Betsy had good taste—and it was all within the guidelines set out by the church.

She sighed. Her clothes were now prepared for this new step. But was she? Lately she had turned the matter over to the Lord again and again, and gradually a sense of anticipation stole into her spirit.

Betsy heard about it first. There was a Saturday afternoon gathering at Ammon Webers, a farm scarcely a mile away. The young men were to help Ammon flail his grain in the barn. It had been gathered into shelter before winter, but the flailing process proved to be more than he could get done alone. So the invitation was out for the young people who relished a working bee. Meanwhile the girls would gather indoors to knit the thick woolen outer socks worn by many to keep their feet warm upon the drafty plank floors of their homes. This way everyone would get something useful done while they socialized.

Betsy proposed the plan cautiously to Susannah. "This sounds like a good place to start, I think. You can knit as well as anyone. My girls need more of those slippers for this winter. And it's close enough that you can walk. Why don't you go?"

"Could we get the Saturday work done in time?" Susannah asked, trying to stall one more time.

"Ach, ya! Mary is a big help already. And you can help bathe the little girls when you get back. That way you can tell me all about it!" Betsy had it all figured out.

Susannah yielded. She'd go if the weather held out.

The weather did. Saturday was cold but sunny.

As she prepared, Susannah's insides felt as shaky as an undercooked hasty pudding. Her parcel of knitting needles and spools of woolen yarn was all ready and wrapped. She combed her long, thick, dark hair as usual. It seemed as if her fingers were clumsy today. She began to despair of ever getting her bun subdued tight enough so her covering would fit properly.

Finally it was done. There was nothing to do but leave. She bade a trembling farewell to Betsy and the girls. She hadn't gone far before she realized she was grateful to be bundled up warmly. The wind attempted to cut through her shawl and coat. It tore at her bundle of yarn—and heightened the tension in her mind.

She'd been to the Weber farm before on errands. *If it's too bad,* she decided, *I'll just never go again. Betsy can say what she wants.*

With this resolve she knocked on the front door.

Mrs. Weber met her with a smiley greeting. "Susannah! Come on in! Did you come to knit?"

"Ya," Susannah said shakily.

"Well, good! Hang your coat up there. Then go on into the front room. That's where they're knitting." Mrs. Weber bustled back to the kitchen.

Susannah clutched her yarn and needles so tightly that her knuckles turned white. She could hear the visiting in the room. Her face felt flushed as she entered.

For a moment the chatter ceased. Susannah's eyes darted around the room. She spied a chair in the corner and headed there.

A few of the girls recognized her with "hellos." In a few minutes talk around the circle resumed. Minutes passed before Susannah relaxed. She unwrapped her spool of homespun yarn and positioned her needles. The girl seated next to her was talking with another girl across the room. On her left sat Martha Gingerich. Susannah sometimes spoke with her on Sundays. Now Martha turned an open smile upon Susannah.

"What were you planning to knit?" she asked, her voice friendly.

"Betsy says her girls need more slippers," Susannah replied.

"Oh, yes. With growing feet in a house, she'll need plenty," Martha agreed.

"What are you making?" Susannah directed the question away from herself.

"Slippers for Mother," Martha said.

Susannah concentrated on her stitches and the needles in her hands. Once a project was started, it didn't require as much attention.

Needles clicked about the room. Talk swirled around her. Susannah didn't know the names of all the girls in the group, but they all seemed to be ordinary young women just like herself. Just now there was a lively discussion on a new technique in making slippers. Susannah found herself enjoying the conversation. Perhaps Betsy was right. These gatherings could be fun.

Susannah carefully counted the stitches she made. When she reached the desired amount, she took another wary look at her companions. All were engrossed in knitting or purling their yarn into useful, warm slippers. At times, one of the more witty girls of the group made a remark that sent ripples of laughter into their midst.

No one was more surprised than Susannah when Mrs. Weber announced to the group that the men were done and were coming in for refreshments.

Susannah followed Martha as the girls hastily grabbed their projects, along with yarn balls and needles. It was proper to let the young men have the sitting room, so the girls moved to the kitchen.

There was a flurry of helping to pour cups of steaming mint tea, and a platter of gingerbread appeared. From the front room a shuffle arose as the room filled with young men who'd been helping Mr. Weber in the barn.

Again Susannah sought a corner from which she could observe the goings on. She blew upon her cup of hot tea, wishing she could disappear in the steam that arose from it. She knew almost none of the young men. Keeping her eyes downcast when they filed into the kitchen for their refreshments seemed safest. When they retreated to the front room, she once again dared to look about. She was glad Betsy had briefed her on the likely pattern of things. She took a tentative sip of tea. Oh, it hit the spot! Its warmth spread into her and gradually the chill of nervousness melted away to the edges.

Martha offered her a piece of gingerbread. Susannah accepted. Its spicy taste was an excellent companion to the hot tea.

Suddenly a scuffle arose from the front room. As one, the girls' heads turned to the interruption. What were the men, or "boys," doing?

Two had entered the kitchen where the girls were clustered around the kitchen table.

A third one followed. "Girls," he announced mischievously. "John and William want to say good-bye to all of you. Next week they head back home to Iowa." He drawled out the last word slowly, then ducked back to the other room where his comrades chuckled merrily.

The two boys standing in the doorway looked at each other for a moment. With a small grin, the darker one of the pair shrugged at his companion, then stepped toward the girl nearest him and offered a handshake.

Several girls tittered. Susannah froze. They were actually going to shake hands with every girl in the room! What nerve!

That was just what they were doing. The taller, dark-haired young man took the lead, followed by his companion of lighter hair. Susannah didn't know which was William or which was John.

She observed closely that a few friendly words were exchanged with each handshake around the circle of young ladies in the room. Maybe this was normal then. The one in the lead must be William, she decided, by something someone said to him.

They had reached Martha now, and then they were upon Susannah.

"Vee gates?" the first young man asked as Susannah stretched out her hand.

She could form no words.

The second young man was right behind. Susannah felt her face must be as red as a live coal in the stove.

He reached to shake her hand. "Who's this?" he asked softly. "Someone new?"

Numbly she received the handshake as she answered briefly, "Susannah Heckendorn." She expected a scornful look at this, for everyone knew the Heckendorn plight. Instead the expression in his hazel eyes was only kind.

They continued to the few remaining girls, then rejoined the other young men in the front room.

Several girls gathered empty teacups and stacked them on the cupboard shelf, while someone produced a songbook. Soon the boys filed quietly into the kitchen again. They lined up along a wall, and a leader called out a song number. There weren't enough songbooks for nearly everyone. Susannah and Martha stood in a group of girls who were without.

A voice lifted up and began the song, then others joined in. Susannah relaxed. It was "Come Thou Fount of Every Blessing." She knew it well. Mentally she blessed Betsy's excellent teaching as she lifted her voice and blended in with the song.

The Weber kitchen rang with melody as exuberant young voices were lifted in praise to God. A few more hymns were selected and sung.

Before she was ready, someone noted the time on the kitchen clock. With an inward gasp, Susannah realized the afternoon was nearly gone. The parting song was chosen. As she joined in singing it, she found that the words matched the feeling in her heart. She certainly needed the Lord's blessing and keeping in her life, and now she also sincerely wished it for each one in this group, even though she didn't know many of them.

At the close of the song, the group dispersed in a flurry of collecting wraps. Good-byes were said in good-natured voices.

Warmly bundled again, Susannah began her walk home. The sun would soon set, and the wind was sharper. She inhaled the brisk air deeply. It felt wonderful.

She stepped up her pace. It would certainly be interesting to recount the afternoon's happenings to Betsy.

chapter 16

Susannah's Longings

Betsy indeed wanted to know all about Susannah's afternoon.
Though she herself was deep in the world of babies, diapers, and
child raising, she maintained a keen interest in community doings.

Susannah related to her how the two young men had said their good-
byes to the group and were leaving soon to return to Iowa.

"Who were they?" Betsy asked curiously.

"I don't know. One was named John and the other William." This was
truly all Susannah knew.

"Hmmm." Betsy's expression showed she was thinking fast. "Oh!
That would be Jacob and Anna Brubaker's son John. You know, they
moved to Iowa ten years ago. I'd heard that their son was back for a
visit, but I'd forgotten it. Now who might William have been? You say
he's also from Iowa?"

"That's what I understood," Susannah said.

"Hmmm. I wonder if they came looking for partners?" Betsy shot a
keen look at Susannah.

"How would I know?" Susannah retorted. If Betsy was going to get
this kind of notion already, Susannah felt maybe she should just stay
home from gatherings. Well, Betsy had nothing to worry about on her

account. No one really knew her. That was beside the point. If they found out she was a Heckendorn, that would settle it. And if that wasn't enough, there was always her nose. It had remained crooked after the fateful day it had been broken. No one would ever look twice at a girl with a nose like this.

Now that the first nerve-wracking attendance with the youth gathering was over, Susannah found herself rather looking forward to attending again. Why, she really hadn't known what she was missing! Even though most of the others were younger than her own twenty-three years, she had enjoyed their company.

Throughout the winter she didn't attend frequently. The weather was usually the deciding factor. In the coldest part of the season no one ventured out unless it was an emergency. It wasn't worth risking your life in the sub-zero temperature, especially with a wind that could cut straight through layers of wraps. Besides, a blizzard could come up out of the north with little warning. The hazards were real enough that wintertime attendance at the meetinghouse was likewise sporadic.

Here at Betsy's home, Susannah no longer minded being cooped up indoors. The noise of Betsy's brood could become clamorous indeed. But no longer did she feel trapped in a home where she was unable to do anything right, and she didn't fear for her own safety as she had in the last few years in the Martin home. Being free from that terrible strain was a tremendous relief to Susannah. It made her want to do all in her power to be a blessing to Betsy.

When the regular household work was done, she gathered yarn balls and knitting needles with zeal. The little ones were growing fast. There was a never-ending need for mittens, scarves, slippers, and stockings. Susannah's needles clicked away the winter hours. The spinning wheel stayed nearly as busy. Its gentle whirring sound was barely heard above the general commotion. Long, ticklish rovings were spun into spool after spool of useful woolen yarn. These could then be dyed or left in the natural woolen color.

Winter finally relented, and the snow slowly began to melt. It was time to collect maple sap and cook it into delicious syrup or brown sugar.

This provided excellent opportunity for working bees for the young folks. Spirits ran high. Once more a fresh, new spring had come. There was new life, and soft, clean air to replace the staleness of a worn-out winter. Susannah attended the gatherings once more at Betsy's urging. Some of the youth had become couples over the winter and a few were planning marriage.

Susannah wondered what that would be like. The thought of having one's own home was pleasant to her, but she doubted if anyone would ever ask *her* to take that huge step. She was already older than Betsy had been when she and Amos had married, so no doubt she would remain single.

Into Susannah's thoughts popped a face. A rather handsome one at that. In spite of all her stern rebukes to herself, she hadn't been able to quite ignore her attraction to Isaac. He was a young man who attended the gatherings of the Mennonite youth. His family was from the community, but not of the Mennonite faith. Until, or if, he ever became a baptized member of the church, she knew there could never be a future in that direction.

Oh, others had done so, but deep down Susannah knew that if she ever did marry someone, she wanted it to be someone who believed the same things she did.

And who said Isaac would ever ask her? Was she just imagining things because he was handsome and had given her attention in front of everyone else? Usually when a young man did this, it was an indication that he was interested in her—unless he was only a flirt. In that case, she wanted to know it before too much longer. But what did God want for her? And could she truly trust Isaac? The last was a frightening thought to Susannah.

Life had taught her early on that men weren't all the same. Some were kind; others weren't. She had no desire to be caught in a marriage with someone who treated her as she had already been treated. For once one married, there was no walking away if it turned out other than what one had hoped. Susannah knew that on the surface few would guess what she knew to be true about Mr. Martin. With company or at the meetinghouse he appeared quite kind, even jovial. His farm was prosperous. By all appearances, everything was in order.

Susannah was too embarrassed to confide her mixed feelings to anyone, even Betsy. What would she know of Susannah's deep fears and haunting questions? She had met and married Amos quite suddenly and quite willingly. There was no way she could ever make sense of Susannah's past and jumbled inner feelings.

This is what Susannah told herself anyhow. She would just take it all to the Lord again.

In spite of that, and even after confiding her trouble to the Lord in the safety of her bedside prayers in the darkness, Susannah admitted to herself one more thing she did enjoy Isaac's attention. It was a heady feeling to be noticed. Especially after all those years of being a nobody.

What he saw in her, she couldn't guess. But what should she do about it? No answer came from above. Susannah wished for a simple, black and white solution. She wasn't used to making up her own mind even in small things, let alone weighty matters.

Not for the first time, Susannah longed to be close to her mother. Surely that would help. Weren't mothers the ones that other young women went to with their problems? What advice might her own mother have for her?

Susannah knew that was a useless idea. Mother was nearly a stranger. She must not waste time on futile wishing.

She would confide it all to God again and ask for His guidance. Surely He who had created her knew all about her struggles, her longings, and her fears. He could take care of her and arrange things as they should be.

That God indeed heard her and was even now arranging things in a completely new direction never once occurred to Susannah.

chapter 17

A Letter

The last strains of the German hymn hovered a few moments in the room after the final words were sung, and the congregation rose for the benediction. Another Sunday service was over.

Women clustered together in groups to visit. The day was warm and springlike. Young girls spilled out the side door of the meetinghouse.

Susannah didn't quite know what to do with herself. Betsy mingled with the married women and mothers. Their conversations didn't stray far from their worlds of raising children. Even though she now knew the girls in the youth group, at times Susannah felt like the odd one. She was older than most of them, and sometimes their lighthearted chatter grated on her more mature nature. Today was such a time.

At last she decided to go sit on Amos and Betsy's wagon. Surely they'd soon be ready to leave for home. She seated herself on the back seat of the wagon to wait.

It was a lovely day. Birds twittered and warbled happily from perches among the new leaves that decked the trees. The sun's rays congenially warmed the air. Susannah could hear the trickle of the creek as it traveled to the larger Conestoga River.

From the corner of her eye she noticed a man approaching the team.

She paid no attention. It would be Amos to untie the horses. Then they could go home.

But the man didn't walk toward the horses' heads. Instead he approached the wagon and faced Susannah. It wasn't Amos.

Susannah's eyes met the sober face. Why, it was Uncle Christian Heckendorn! Her startled mind registered the man's appearance even as he greeted her.

She returned his "hello" shyly. After all, she barely knew the man. What could he want with her?

He didn't keep her waiting long. "I was in town last week," he began slowly. "When I picked up our mail at the store, there was a letter there for you."

Susannah was speechless.

"I figured it best to give it to you here," he continued. With that he stretched forth his hand toward her.

Her startled gaze took in the name written in a scrawl across the front of the envelope— "Susannah Heckendorn." She reached for it dumbly. Who would be writing to her? And why? It was from the United States, according to the stamp affixed in the top, right-hand corner.

She was too busy trying to fathom why anyone would send her a letter to notice the keen glance her uncle directed to her face.

"What does this mean?" he asked slowly.

"Not much," Susannah muttered. She slipped it under her light shawl. No matter what it contained, she'd wait to open it until she had privacy.

Without further ado her uncle turned to leave.

Susannah's mind spun in circles but arrived at no conclusions. She was relieved when Betsy and the children finally left the visiting folks at the meetinghouse and climbed aboard the wagon. She was even more relieved that Betsy hadn't seemed to notice her brief conversation with Uncle Christian. That way she didn't have to deal with questions she didn't know how to answer.

Finally Amos was done visiting. He untied the horses and they headed swiftly toward home. It seemed to Susannah one of the longest rides she could recall. The letter nearly seemed to melt against her bosom where she'd slipped it out of sight of prying eyes. Letters were only for important news—news that was worth the ridiculous price of a stamp. Never had she gotten one. What could it be?

Once at home, Betsy was busy getting the children unwrapped and settled. It was Susannah's job to set the table and prepare the simple lunch they'd have. The letter would have to wait.

Had anyone noticed, they might have wondered at her quietness. She didn't have much to contribute to the talk around the table.

Betsy was full of talk, however, and kept the conversation going. Once in a while Susannah needed to answer, but she did so without elaborating.

At last the meal was over. Susannah helped clear the table. Betsy's oldest two daughters usually did the noon dishes.

Finally Susannah felt free to head upstairs. Hastily she gathered her bonnet and shawl, in the pretense of needing to put them away. As swiftly as she dared, she darted up the narrow stairs.

Her breath came quickly. A strange feeling stole over her. It was as if something new had come her way—something that might indicate a change.

She slit the envelope with her hairpin. There was one folded paper inside. Her eyes scanned it hastily. The words didn't quite register in her shocked mind. She read the signature.

John Brubaker.

She read the letter again. There wasn't much to it. Then she looked at the name once more. Why, that was the John she'd seen at her first time with the young folks! One of the two who'd shaken hands with all the girls. He'd been leaving to return to Iowa. The letter was from Iowa. She turned it over slowly and stared dumbly at the envelope again.

That meant...

Again she read the short letter. He was asking for a courtship with her! Someone had actually asked Susannah Heckendorn! It was all too strange.

Her mind scrambled wildly. How was she to answer this question? She willed her heart to stop beating so fast. It was making her dizzy.

What about…what about Isaac? Her mind flew to the face of the young man who had occupied too much of her thoughts lately. She groaned.

This was someone from far away. Someone she'd only seen once. How was she to know what to do? Ach, why did this have to come along to confuse her? And just what did this John know of her anyway? How could he know he wished to spend time with her when he'd only seen her once?

What if she agreed to seeing him? Suppose he asked her to move with him to Iowa, a place so far away it wasn't even in Canada. The thought was too much.

Why did the odd feeling persist that this might be part of God's plan? That maybe this was the answer He sent when she'd begged for wisdom about Isaac? John was already a member of the church. Isaac was not, and might never be.

As all these facts registered slowly in Susannah's mind, it seemed a bit clearer to her tumbling thoughts what she should do.

Besides, Isaac hadn't actually asked her. Maybe he was a flirt and never would.

chapter 18

Susannah's Answer

Susannah suffered indecision for several days. This thing had descended upon her with the suddenness of a winter blizzard. She was unprepared for such a major decision. At night she lay awake, pondering John's request. The thought of what might lie ahead if she agreed to his question scared her. Then, as if driven by an opposing freakish wind, came the chilling fear that if she declined this opportunity, she might never have another chance. This might be the only man who'd ever ask her.

From what she'd gathered among the young girls, not many passed up on an offer to date. Most seemed to think that "a trout in the pot is better than a salmon in the sea." Unconsciously Susannah now applied this pet phrase of Amos's to her situation.

Finally she took the matter to Betsy. Perhaps she'd have advice.

"Well, now!" Betsy was clearly pleased. "My, aren't you glad now you can read and write?" she teased.

"Ach, you!" Susannah felt her face flush. "I didn't tell you this so you can laugh at me."

"Oh, I know." Betsy sobered, but her eyes still sparkled. "You know, that family is rather nice. Mrs. Jacob Brubaker, John's mother, once had your sister Franey to work for her, didn't she?"

"Yes," Susannah agreed. "She would always bring along a pretty dish for Franey whenever she went to town."

"Umm." Betsy looked thoughtful. Then she said, "You could certainly do worse. But he's from Iowa! I wonder if he'd expect you to move there too?"

"I'm afraid of that," Susannah admitted. "But he hasn't asked to marry me! Just for courtship. Maybe I'm worrying ahead of time."

"But if he wrote a letter, he must be serious!" Betsy stated the obvious. "Why, I never even got such a letter!"

Susannah blushed again. Then she sighed. It felt good to have shared with Betsy. But the decision still remained to be made.

"I can't tell you what to do," Betsy finally said. "But it sounds like a good opportunity to me. I wouldn't keep him waiting too long. That wouldn't be very nice."

"Humph," Susannah almost snorted. "This business of making up my mind can't be done overnight. I have a notion to take as long as I need."

And this she did.

Many times she turned the matter over to God, asking Him for direction. Always the peculiar conviction descended upon her that this was God's direction. Susannah couldn't shake the feeling that in some mysterious way, God had introduced the beginning of her future by means of John's letter.

Ever since she'd taken the first shaky step of faith in God, she'd tried to listen to the quiet voice of her conscience. Once in a sermon she'd heard that God often directed His people by that small voice of reason He had placed within each soul. If so, then she had better not refuse this offer. Just suppose it really was what God had in store for her life? If He had provided for her needs so far, why would He quit now?

Finally her mind accepted what her conscience was telling her. Even though she didn't know what the future held, she would accept John's offer. Then she would wait to see how God would work it all out.

Watching for a chance when the little ones weren't all listening, she informed Betsy of her decision.

Betsy's joy at hearing this news was contagious. "Let's see," she offered. "Would you like to send a letter along the next time we go to town?"

"Yes," Susannah said, "I suppose I should."

Saying it aloud to someone made it seem final. She calmed her racing thoughts now by reasoning that there was still plenty of time to get that letter written. The trip to town wouldn't be for a while yet.

And mail to the States was slow. She had no idea how far John would need to go to get his mail, nor how often it might arrive in that rural settlement of Iowa.

Right now, the thought that communication between them would be slow and infrequent was a comforting thought. That meant there wouldn't be any huge changes in her comfortable life just yet.

Her twenty-fourth birthday had come and gone. Summer brought with it longer daylight hours. It also brought long hours of hard work. Again there was no idle time on the farm. The raising and preserving food for Betsy's household was a serious task. There was kraut to be cut and salted. Great briny crocks of it would be packed away. Corn to be cut and dried. Beans to pick and shell. There was always laundry, for Betsy liked her children to be kept clean.

Always there was the extra cooking and baking for hired men and harvest laborers.

Late summer and autumn again brought bushels of juicy, crisp apples. These must be picked and gathered. Some were snitzed and dried for winter use. The large iron kettle was set up outdoors. Gallons of cider and apple chunks were cooked together with brown sugar. The rich, mellow apple butter was a family favorite.

It seemed to Susannah that the autumn passed by even quicker than the summer. Winter was just around the corner, and the New Year loomed just ahead. It wasn't just any New Year, but the turn of the century. Once January arrived it would be the year 1900. That was strange. It didn't even sound right. All she'd ever known was 18 something. What might lurk in such a significant year?

No one but God could know. So the only thing to do was what she'd always done—trust God and take one day at a time.

chapter 19

The Third Letter

The year 1900 started like many others before it, with an ordinary day. Susannah had a premonition though that it really wouldn't be an ordinary year for her. John Brubaker had written another letter to her and had made it quite clear that he was serious in his interest of her. Susannah couldn't deny that this still amazed her.

The reality of it warmed her heart. Maybe she wasn't such an unwanted creature after all. In her own family she was nearly a stranger to her siblings as well as her parents. Then in the Martin home... She shuddered as memories crowded against a door she preferred to keep shut. Well, Betsy had been a Godsend, that much was sure. Yet even there, at times Susannah felt like a misfit, an extra cog on a wheel that might have revolved just fine without her.

Now to be chosen like this, by a young man who had intentions for a future... It looked big to Susannah. Big and special, but scary.

It wasn't long before another change came into her life. Her oldest brother Moses became interested in land south of the border in the state of Michigan. He and his wife Amanda by now had three small daughters. The oldest, Arclista, was six years old. She was followed by Luella and Alta.

Moses was quite eager to begin the heavy work of clearing his new property, and word reached Susannah that he had already left Ontario with their possessions and livestock. Amanda and the girls were to leave in a week or so, also on the train.

The news left a hollow spot in Susannah's heart. She really didn't know them that well. Still, it had been a comfort to know that her family was all somewhere in the home community. It made Susannah feel homesick just to know that they were now scattered farther apart.

Who knew what changes life might yet bring? Susannah wished she could reach out and halt the hands of time. What if she herself ended up moving far away? The thought wouldn't stay in the back of her mind.

February brought sad news from Michigan. Amanda had indeed taken the girls and left on the train to meet Moses at their new property. Enroute the girls contracted the dreaded diphtheria and became very sick.

Amanda decided to get off the train in Port Huron and stay with an uncle there until the girls recovered.

God had other plans. After days of intense suffering, Arclista died.

Susannah's heart ached for her little niece who had suffered so much. She also hurt for her sister-in-law Amanda. There had been nothing for Amanda to do but send a telegram to Moses, telling him the sad news. Due to the quarantine, no funeral could be held. The child was laid to rest in a lonely cemetery in Port Huron on a cruelly cold winter's day.

Why did life have to be so sad? Susannah could not imagine the grief of her brother and his wife at this turn of events. Were parents always to live in the dread of a sickness snatching away their children? Would she someday be in those shoes? The thought was sobering. Could she do it? Would she be strong enough to stand that test if it should ever come her way?

Soon after this Susannah had a chance meeting with her younger sister, Lydiann.

"Why, Susannah," greeted Lydiann cheerfully. "I'm glad to see you. I have news. Or have you heard?"

"No, what now?" Susannah asked almost warily. Was there more bad news in her family?

"I'm getting married!" Lydiann announced.

"Oh!" Susannah raised her eyebrows in question. "That's good news. To whom?"

"Fred Mulholland," Lydiann replied with a bright sparkle in her eye.

The idea of this bright young creature being her own sister made Susannah a bit slow in responding.

"Where will you live?" she asked.

"At Branchton," Lydiann bubbled. "Do you know where that is?"

"No," Susannah admitted. "I don't get around much."

"It's a village just south of Galt."

"I'm glad you're not moving far away like Moses did," Susannah commented.

"Me too," Lydiann sobered. "What about you, Susannah? Are you ever going to marry?"

Susannah felt her face heat up. "I'm getting letters from a young man," she admitted.

"Oh! Where's he from?" Lydiann was instantly curious. "Do I know him?"

"From Iowa, Susannah replied.

"Iowa!" Lydiann gasped. "Susannah! Not one of those goody-goodys who started that real plain church?" Her tone dripped with disgust.

Susannah bristled inwardly. "He didn't start the church," she retorted. "But yes, he's from the group that moved away from here in 1888. He was just a boy then. They can't be so much different from us."

"See if I'd marry someone who wants to be so awkwardly plain and behind the times," Lydiann murmured. "But best wishes just the same."

Later, Susannah couldn't recall with what words they had parted. Her sister's remarks still stung. Was that what people really thought of the Iowa community? Was John a goody-goody?

Susannah faced the fact squarely. She didn't know him well enough to know.

By spring she received her third letter from John. Its contents turned her spirit inside out, leaving her in a turmoil from which she couldn't imagine a way out.

In the letter John asked if she would marry him. He also asked if she would come halfway. Would she meet him in Chicago, then they could get married right away?

chapter 20

A Brave Reply

The nerve! Once she could breathe again Susannah was nearly angry. What did he think she was? If he thought she was going to get on a train and leave the country to marry a man she'd only met once, then he'd better think again! Why, she had a notion to write to him and let him know that he could just find someone else.

Susannah groaned within. What was she going to do? Why did she have to be faced with so many decisions? Was there anyone who could tell her what to do?

Into her mind flew her last meeting with sister Lydiann. She'd been radiant with joy at the mere mention of her upcoming marriage. Apparently she had no such doubts as this. *Why do I have to be the one involved in such a ridiculous courtship as this?* Susannah asked herself.

While she gradually calmed down, Susannah found her thoughts fleeing back to her only meeting with John. Always when she did this, she could vividly picture the kind expression on his face. Even in his eyes. It was the only memory that consoled her. Surely, surely, with such an expression, a man wouldn't turn out to be cruel and untrustworthy, would he? As she pondered these things, aggravation gave way to fear, and her thoughts became stormy and muddled. She nearly felt sick to her stomach as past happenings and a feeling of panic threatened to overwhelm her.

At last she realized this was getting her nowhere. Giving in to the darkness of the past had never helped before and it wouldn't now either.

She would talk to Betsy. That usually soothed her somehow.

Susannah slid the letter into her drawer with the previous two. For a moment she gazed at them. How could those three innocent-looking envelopes have caused her such trouble? Her life had been fine before they arrived, hadn't it? She pondered a moment on the fact that it lay in her power to end it all. If she refused John's request, the turmoil it caused her would be over. She took a deep breath. That would be nice in a way. Then she could go on and enjoy the gatherings with the young folks with no reservations.

And yet… Susannah's eyes took on a faraway gleam. Yet she wouldn't be the same again. Not quite. The whole experience had matured her and made it even harder for her to fit in with the carefree youth. If she did decline the proposal, how would she ignore the conviction that had always assured her that this was what God wanted of her? Could it be that even this sudden turn of events had God's approval?

Susannah closed the drawer. There was no doubt that God had given her peace once she had accepted John's first offer. Peace from her own selfish hankerings that focused on the attraction of a young man who wasn't settled, and might never settle. But would that same peace cover a clandestine wedding such as John now asked for?

She turned and went downstairs. If there was a good chance, she'd talk with Betsy.

Susannah busied herself with work while she waited for a chance. Finally it was chore time. Betsy reminded her daughters that it was time to gather eggs. Once they were safely out the door and a distance away, Susannah turned to Betsy.

"John wrote and asked me to marry him." She didn't mince words.

Betsy faced her. "Well! I thought he might. I just didn't expect it so soon."

"He asked me to meet him in Chicago. Then we could get married before harvest."

It was amusing to watch Betsy's jaw drop. Her eyes became nearly as round as her mouth. She stared at Susannah for a moment.

"This summer?" she gasped.

"Yes, that's what he's thinking," Susannah said in a tone much calmer than she felt.

"Well!" Betsy exclaimed again. "That part is a surprise. Will you be going soon, then?"

"I don't know what to do." Susannah decided on honesty. "He has some nerve to ask such a thing. I've half a notion to call the whole thing quits."

Betsy looked doubtful. "If you did that, who knows, he might ask someone else. Then what about you?"

Susannah shrugged.

"Have you prayed?" came Betsy's next question.

"I've done plenty, since the whole thing started," Susannah confirmed.

"Keep on," Betsy advised. "Some wisdom is sure to come if you ask for it." She paused. After a moment of silence she added in a low voice. "You should think long and hard before you refuse. But the choice is yours."

Susannah groaned. "Yes, the choice is mine. That's what makes it so hard." Then in a moment she added, "Neither would I want anyone else to choose for me. I just need someone to help me figure out what to do."

The conversation ended, but Betsy's question, "Then what about you" kept echoing through Susannah's mind. No doubt there would be someone else John could and would marry if she refused. Men hardly ever stayed single. Iowa surely wasn't such a deserted place that it had no eligible women. If he were a decent sort of man at all, then he could likely find a woman willing to marry him out there. One whom he could court and wed without such a long trip, if that was his problem.

If Susannah was honest with herself, she had to admit she had almost been looking forward to marrying John, should he ask. But this was too much.

Why, she'd hardly ever been to town! And he was asking her to travel to Chicago on the train. He had no idea what he was asking of her!

But then she thought again about Betsy's question— "What about you?" *Indeed, what about me?* Susannah asked herself. How would she really like it if John married someone else?

Once again, she was glad no one was going to town in the next day or so. That would give her time to think and pray.

By the time Amos and Betsy needed supplies, Susannah had her answer ready.

On the morning they were to leave for town, she handed Betsy a sealed envelope to mail for her. It was addressed to John Brubaker, May City, Iowa.

chapter 21

Waiting

Betsy didn't question Susannah on the contents. When they arrived home from the village, she merely said, "I mailed your letter. It should be on its way as soon as the next mail goes out."

"Thank you," Susannah said simply. She busied herself. That wasn't hard to do in this household. She'd learned a long time ago that work, and plenty of it, was an excellent tonic for unwanted thoughts and fears.

She had plenty of both now that she'd sent her answer. It was now out of her control. She had answered the best she could, with all the wisdom she'd been able to summon. Now it was up to John—and God. For she had sent her response in what she believed was God's will.

Try as she might, Susannah couldn't keep her dispirited thoughts at bay. They stalked her no matter how industriously she worked…

Betsy wasn't blind. After a week of watching the younger woman behave as though she were driven, she opened the subject politely.

"Can you share what's bothering you?" she asked when there was a private opportunity.

"Ach," Susannah's face reddened. "I'm just silly. I keep wondering what John's going to do next."

Betsy surveyed her calmly. "What do you mean?" she asked finally.

"When he gets the letter I sent. I just wonder what he'll do about it," Susannah replied.

"What did you write to him?" Betsy asked cautiously.

"I told him I would marry him, but I won't come to Chicago to meet him. I told him I think we should have a decent church wedding." Susannah said this slowly. "Surely I'm worth that much."

Betsy made a curious little sound. It was a half gasp and half snort. "You wrote that to him?" she asked dubiously.

"Ya," Susannah admitted. "And if he doesn't want to come all the way up here, he can just go marry someone else."

"But aren't you afraid he might do just that?" Betsy obviously thought Susannah had done it all wrong.

Susannah hung her head a few seconds. "In a way I am," she said softly.

"So there won't be a summer wedding?" Betsy asked bluntly.

"Not unless he shows up," Susannah reaffirmed. "If he does come, I think he'll wait till after harvest. That's the reason he wanted me to meet him in Chicago. He has too much work in summer to take a long trip."

"What will you do if he doesn't come?" Betsy asked.

Susannah shrugged. "I'll wait and see," she said with more confidence than she felt. This was the anxiety that had driven her ever since she'd mailed her answer. What if John decided she really wasn't worth the trouble? Maybe he thought she was stubborn or selfish. Had she risked too much for her conviction and her desire for a real wedding? Now that her answer was on its way, the truth stared her boldly in the face. A future as a single woman no longer appealed to her, but maybe that was exactly what she had brought upon herself.

Well, she thought, *I did it because I believed it was God's will. Now I'll wait and see if it is.* With this little reminder to herself, her doubts scurried to the far corners of her mind again.

It was a relief to have Betsy know the situation. In fact, Betsy seemed to realize Susannah's need to stay occupied.

As more people had moved into the area in recent years, most chose to live in or close to town. There they could work by day in woolen factories, brickyards, or other industries. These people bought almost all their food, so farmers in the area had started selling their excess crops to these people.

Betsy decided this was something Susannah could do. She encouraged her to gather extra wild fruits and berries in her spare time. These could be taken along and peddled when they went to town for supplies.

Susannah was eager. She spent countless hours scouring the back fields and wood lanes for wild huckleberries, raspberries, or blackberries.

As Betsy said, if she did marry, the bit of extra money would surely come in handy to buy household goods. And if she didn't, it could be saved for a rainy day.

So Susannah struggled with thorny briers and aggravating bush flies in the thickets as she picked bucketfuls of nature's jewels. Out here among the wild things, soaking in the warm sunshine and breathing deeply of fresh, clean air, there was less likelihood of her thoughts hindering her work. Here, alone, it didn't matter if her thoughts did stray. They might even stray as far away as Iowa if they wanted.

This they did, for she still had no reply to the letter she'd sent to John.

Would her future lie far away in the prairies of Iowa? Would this be her last summer in Ontario? If so, what would it be like in Iowa?

Faintly she recalled rumors of Indian attacks in that area of Iowa. Those tales had circulated freely during the years when the first families from here had moved to that state. Was it still a land of wild, lawless Indians? There hadn't been a chance to ask John if there was any truth to those stories.

Susannah shuddered in spite of the warm breeze. Just the idea of such an attack made her blood run cold. Of course, Ontario had its own Indian history and some of it wasn't pleasant. Susannah couldn't help but wonder if things might not have gone better if the white settlers had treated the Indians fairly and with Christian goodwill. There was nothing to do about it now. The dealings had been done before her time.

Another thing that worried her was that she knew no one in Iowa. Most of the families living there had come from here to start with. But at that time the only meager contact she'd had with anyone was at the meetinghouse on Sundays. The thought of being a complete stranger in a relatively new settlement didn't appeal to her at all. Why, the only person she'd know was John!

With this, another thought followed on its heels. Did she even know John? Susannah admitted to herself that she really didn't. Yes, there would be time to get to know him after they were married. But what if he wasn't the kind of person she believed him to be? Again she shuddered in the warm sunlight.

She glanced at her surroundings. The afternoon shadows were growing long. Her pail was full enough.

Susannah gave herself a mental shake. Who said there was going to be a wedding? John might never come.

chapter 22

Preparations

Autumn's chill winds were driving the spent leaves from the trees when the long-awaited letter from John arrived. Susannah held it in her hands in the privacy of her room. She turned it over several times before opening it. "Lord," she breathed, "help me face whatever this letter may contain."

Finally she slit it open and withdrew the thin paper. She felt as vulnerable as the leafless trees outside. Her future hung on this one piece of paper. What might it hold?

Never having written a wordy letter, John didn't do so now. With a few simple sentences he acknowledged that he'd received her letter. In another few sparse sentences he stated his intentions of being in Canada again in the near future. They could then become married, and soon afterward they would move to Iowa. That way he could be there in plenty of time to get the spring work started on the land he planned to farm.

There were a few more details, but Susannah couldn't absorb them now. With a start she realized she'd been holding her breath. She exhaled deeply to release her built-up tension. He had actually waited for her! And was coming in person! That meant their wedding could be here in familiar territory. Susannah's relief came from deep within her heart. She'd given him the freedom to choose otherwise, and he'd chosen to be faithful to her. He still wanted her!

Her thoughts stumbled over each other in a half dozen directions at once. Some were bright and lively with joy. Others were darker and tinged with fear. Susannah wasn't a starry-eyed girl like her sister Lydiann had been when they'd met earlier this year. Her life had held struggles, sickness, and hardships up until now, and she didn't expect that to change after she married.

But right now her heart was so full that she felt the need to tell someone. Betsy! She must find Betsy, her only close friend, and tell her that John was going to come.

She arose to take the stairs down to the kitchen. Suddenly she felt shy about sharing this news. So far it belonged only to John and herself. Once she shared it, it would be private no more.

"Ach, Betsy deserves to know," she muttered. Then she went downstairs.

As Susannah expected, Betsy was pleased with the news. "I was afraid you'd lost him for good when you wrote that you wouldn't meet him halfway," she admitted.

Susannah nodded. She had sensed Betsy thought she'd made a grave mistake. Now that it was settled she was more relieved than ever that this was how it was going to be. A peacefulness stole over her. She had obeyed her conscience, and God had proved that it had been the right thing to do. Surely she could also trust Him to lead her into the future.

Betsy soon began making plans for the upcoming wedding.

"Let's see," she began, with a gleam in her eyes that Susannah recognized as determination. "You'll need a wedding dress, of course. And you'll need dishes too. Why, you'll need everything!"

Susannah chuckled. She entered the plans with a dig of her own this time. "Betsy! If I didn't know better, I'd think you're just glad to get rid of me!"

"Now, come on!" Betsy exclaimed. "You know well enough I'll have to work harder than ever after you go. The girls will have to really buckle up and help. But they're old enough. It'll be hard to see you leave for Iowa; never doubt that."

"I do wish it weren't so far away," Susannah said slowly. "Can I even hope to come back to visit?"

"I suppose that depends on how good a manager John is," Betsy answered. "Such a long trip would certainly dip into the pocketbook."

Susannah nodded. It would be too much to ask. And as a married woman she would no longer have her own money.

A married woman! The thought startled her in its very truth. She, of all people! At least she would no longer be one of the poor Heckendorns. In a way it would be a relief to change her name to Brubaker. Yet deep down in her heart, Susannah felt that she would always remain a Heckendorn. That was, after all, the family God had placed her in.

The weeks leading up to John's arrival by train seemed to fly by. On one hand, Susannah was glad. On the other, she wanted to absorb all the housekeeping knowledge she could while she was still under Betsy's roof. Soon enough she'd have to do things on her own.

Betsy assured her that she had no doubts as to Susannah's ability.

"But I won't be able to ask you for help if I don't know how to do something," Susannah worried.

"What is it you don't know?" Betsy asked.

"Oh, I can't think of anything right now," Susannah said.

"See, you'll be fine," Betsy said with a smile.

Betsy and Amos needed to make a trip to town again. When they came home with the team, Amos unloaded a large crate and carried it gingerly into the house for his beaming wife.

Betsy couldn't contain herself. "Here, Susannah," she announced. "See if you like these dishes. They're our gift to you."

Susannah gasped. "For me! Betsy!"

Betsy nodded. Amos was already pulling a board loose from the top of the crate.

As if in a dream, Susannah reached into the opening and fumbled with the packing. Her fingers settled on a piece. Carefully she pulled it out.

She gasped again. No one but Betsy could have chosen as well. The ivory china had a dainty golden rim, with another on the edge. In the center of the plate was a cluster of blue lily-of-the-valleys. Only Betsy had ever known that this was Susannah's favorite flower. She clutched the piece to her heart. With a fervent breath, she said, "Thank you, Amos and Betsy!" But the words sounded so inadequate. How could she ever convey the depths of gratitude she felt for this lovely gift?

"There's plenty more in the crate," Betsy urged. "Go ahead and look at them."

Susannah looked. Sure enough! A matching set, all with that lovely sprig of lily-of-the-valley. In a daze she turned one of the plates upside down. On the bottom was stamped in small letters:

Royal Ironstone China

Johnson Bros.

Late Parkhurst and Co. England.

Real china! For her! What a dear Betsy was! And the fact that she could read those words on the bottom of this precious gift was also to Betsy's credit. Her gratitude knew no bounds as her eyes blurred with happy tears.

This floral pattern was traced directly from an original piece of Susannah's wedding gift dishes, given to her by Betsy. The dishes are owned by her granddaughter, Josephine Stauffer.

chapter 23

The Wedding

It was January 4, 1901, their wedding day. It still seemed unreal to Susannah.

The elderly Bishop Abraham Martin had agreed to come to the house and perform the service. Susannah nearly felt sorry for him that he had to venture outdoors in the dead of winter at his age. But John had made the arrangements and so it was.

She smoothed her dark hair and made sure her covering was on straight. A glance downward across the warm fabric of her new brown dress assured her that on the outside at least, she was ready. She might as well go downstairs.

John was there already. She greeted him as if in a daze. Was it really true? This man and she were to share their lives from now on—for as long as God granted them living breath. Her thoughts were in such a jumble that none of them made much sense. Her gaze sought John's eyes. Ah, yes. It was still there. The warm, kind look that had been there the first time she'd met him. It calmed her tattered nerves.

"I believe that is Abraham's team coming now," announced Betsy. She bustled about the kitchen, busily adding more wood to the hungry stove. She was making the day as special as she could, and she wanted the kitchen to be cozy for this special event.

Amos helped to stable Abraham's team in the barn, then a few minutes later he ushered him into the house.

Betsy arranged the chairs for the simple ceremony. Thoughtfully she placed Abraham's closest to the warm stove, next to the table. There he could place his Bible within easy reach. She placed two more chairs at a slight angle in front of that. These were for John and Susannah. Then she placed one each for herself and Amos behind those. There, everything was ready.

It seemed unreal to Susannah, but soon she and John were seated side by side in front of the bishop. Willing her pounding heart to slow its rapid pace, she listened closely as Abraham began the ceremony. He spoke in German in a serious tone. He reminded them that marriage vows were sacred, second only to the vow one made to follow Jesus Christ. Marriage was created with a divine plan and was not to be entered into lightly.

Susannah soaked up the words intently. A sidewise glance at John proved that he too was giving his full attention. It seemed only moments before Abraham beckoned for them to rise before him. His voice was deep and sober as he asked the vows. Some were directed at John.

John's voice was low and steady as he answered each time with a solemn, "Yes."

When they addressed her, Susannah heard her own voice come forth shakily. She, too, answered each question with her promise.

"Now, clasp your right hands," Abraham directed.

John and Susannah obeyed.

Abraham laid both of his hands on top of their clasped ones and spoke the final blessing. "May the God of Abraham, the God of Isaac, and the God of Jacob go with you and help you. Go forth as husband and wife. Fear God and keep His commandments. I wish you the grace and blessings of God. Amen."

As Susannah reclaimed her seat, the thought flew through her mind that the faithful God of the patriarchs of old was still the same God both she and John sought to serve.

After Bishop Abraham said another prayer the service was over.

Amos and Betsy suggested singing a few hymns yet to fit the occasion. The voices of the few people in the room rang to the rooftop in genuine worship. A few German songs were sung first, then in a soft voice Betsy announced one more she thought they should sing.

Susannah's heart was nearly too full of feelings to join in, but it was her favorite English song. Betsy's clear, sweet voice led out in the words of "The Lily of the Valley." Again, only Betsy would have known that this one was extra special to Susannah. Soon she heard her own voice join and blend in with the others.

When the last strains drifted away, Betsy arose and began the final preparations for the meal she'd planned.

The men soon drifted from the kitchen, feeling out of place now that the ceremony was over.

Susannah set the table with her own new dishes. With her heart nearly bursting, she barely noticed the food that Betsy had so thoughtfully added extra touches to.

After the meal, when the men pushed back their chairs from the table in satisfaction, ordinary small talk circulated.

Eventually Abraham rose to his feet. The marriage license John had produced needed to be signed and dated. This done, Abraham took his wraps and prepared for his homeward journey. It had been a long day for him, and he wished to be home before the early winter twilight caught up with him.

Amos and John brought wooden crates and boxes in from the barn. With mixed feelings Susannah packed the china and her other few belongings carefully into them. Betsy insisted that she take several of the rugs along that she'd braided last winter.

"I'm sure Iowa houses have cold floors too," had been her response to Susannah's protests.

At last she was done. John nailed the tops securely in place. Things were ready for the long journey to Iowa—and her new life.

Part II

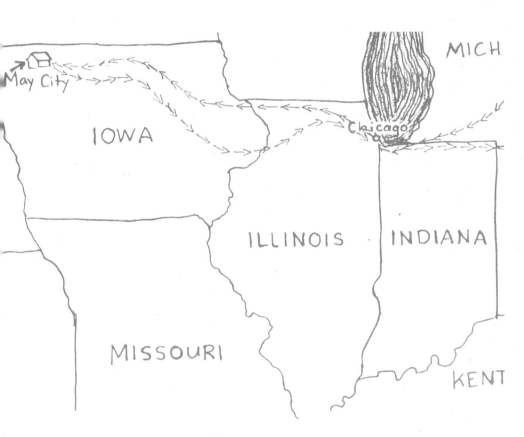

chapter 24

May City, Iowa

"Why, thank you, Mrs. Brubaker," was John's response when Susannah offered him a large red apple from the box of food she'd packed for their long trip. "These are really a special treat."

"Why is that?" she asked.

"Fruit is scarce in Iowa," he responded. "I sure miss all those apples we had when I was a boy."

The train lurched and swayed. The iron wheels beneath them emitted screeches and clacks as they traveled along the steel rails that guided the huge train.

Susannah was at last getting used to the constant motion and noise. When they had first boarded the steam-belching giant at Berlin, her heart had nearly leaped out of her chest. It was bigger than she'd imagined. If it hadn't been for John at her side, guiding her to the right coach and selecting a seat by the window for them, she wouldn't have had the nerve to climb aboard the black monster.

Now, as they steadily clickety-clacked their way to a new beginning, the noises, whistles, and crossing signal toots were becoming familiar. Susannah settled back in her seat again. This was turning out to be a good opportunity to learn more about her new husband. And about the community they would be living in.

"If there's no fruit, then what do you eat?" she asked, voicing her curiosity.

"Oh, there are some wild plum trees by the riverbank. But they're small," John said slowly as he ate his apple. "And mulberries here and there. If you can beat the birds to them."

Susannah listened carefully.

"But if we don't have apples, we certainly do have potatoes," John said with a smile. "Why, here in Canada a man has to roll up his shirtsleeves to even find a potato in his soup!"

He chuckled at the look of amusement in Susannah's eyes.

"What about Indians?" Susannah asked, changing the subject.

"Indians?" John asked.

"Yes. When you folks first left Ontario to move to Iowa, there were lots of stories about all the terrible things going on out on the prairies," Susannah persisted. "Do you still see Indians? Will they still be a threat?"

John was thoughtful. "Iowa has lots of Indian stories," he agreed. "Lots of the lakes, rivers, and towns are named after them. But the only Indians we see these days are civilized ones."

"What about attacks?"

"The last one I know of happened in 1857, about thirty years before we came to the area," John said after a bit. "But it was bad."

"Oh." Susannah wasn't sure she wanted to know, and yet it might be better than ignorance.

"Yes, it is called the Spirit Lake Massacre," John said slowly. "Do you really want to hear about it?"

Susannah nodded.

"Those settlers had come from back East," John began. "They liked the area by the lake, and decided to stay and stake claims. They hurried to build their cabins and settle in before winter came. When winter did come, so did a band of Dakota Indians. This had been their winter campground for many years and they weren't happy to find it now settled by whites. They had named the lake 'Spirit Lake,' and it was a sacred place to them.

"Inkpaduta was their chief's name. He deliberately set up their lodges close to the white men's cabins, hoping to scare them away. It didn't work. The whites were determined to stay put. They had a number of squabbles, and like many times before, the whites took advantage of the Indians in a deal for some straw which the Dakotas wanted." John said this last part in a regretful tone.

Susannah nodded. It was the same old story of whites cheating the Indians. In Ontario it had been the same.

"Then what?"

"Inkpaduta was angry, of course. And still upset about a previous incident, as well," John said sadly. "He saw his chance for revenge. He and his sons and tribesmen went on the warpath and killed forty-two white settlers at the Spirit Lake settlement that March."

"Forty-two!" Susannah gasped.

"Yes. Many were children," John continued. "They also took four white women captive."

"What happened to them?"

"Two were later killed. The other two were bought back by the military and returned to the whites."

Susannah shuddered. The horror was unimaginable. What terror must have beset those women? And yet… "If the white people hadn't been so greedy, things might have gone differently." She spoke her thoughts.

"Yes," John agreed. "The whites brought the Indians' wrath upon themselves. But then the innocent ones had to suffer too."

The couple sat in silence, lost in their own thoughts.

"What else can you tell me about Iowa that might scare me?" Susannah asked at last, teasingly.

"Umm. Let's see." There was a twinkle in John's eyes. "How about tornadoes?"

"What are they?" Susannah asked curiously.

"Oh, a sort of twisting, stormy wind. Sometimes they seem to have suction too. When they're bad, they can lift up entire buildings."

"Ach now, be serious," Susannah rebuked mildly.

"I am," John said. "Once when we hadn't lived there very long, when I was about twelve, we had one. It was a stuffy, windy afternoon. I was up in the barn, throwing hay down to the cattle below when the storm hit. When I climbed down and went toward the house for supper, there was no house there anymore."

"Where was it?"

"The twister had sucked it up and carried it all the way across the field to Chain Lake," John recalled. "About a mile away. Knives and forks were scattered all across the field, for Mother had been making supper."

"What happened to her?" Susannah asked.

"When she heard the roar coming, she quickly went to the cellar. She always says she prayed like never before while she was down there," John said. "God answered her prayers, for none of us were hurt. We were able to repair the house."

"Do those storms come often?" Susannah couldn't help but ask.

"Not really. But once in a while is plenty!" John replied.

Susannah pondered in silence. Had she really agreed to move to a place where Indians slaughtered white folks by the dozen and where strange storms carried away whole houses?

The sun was setting in the west. A glare shone upon the train window beside her seat. Onward, ever onward, the train was carrying them through the twilight. Each clack and lurch brought her closer to that land where she was to make her new home—a place that held spine-tingling incidents like the ones John had just told her of.

chapter 25

A New Beginning

"Where are the trees?" Susannah asked. They were nearing Iowa. She anxiously observed the landscape for anything that might give a hint of hominess.

"There aren't many," John answered. "Just small scrubby stuff along the streams. Anything else gets burned by the wildfires."

Susannah didn't voice her dismay. No trees! What would there be to shelter homes with? No strong, large, friendly trees? It was unthinkable. Yet it must be so. The landscape rushing by outside the train windows couldn't exactly be called flat. There were gentle knolls and valleys, with little winding streams here and there. Snow and ice covered much of the land. Interspersed were tall, coarse blades of frozen grass. But there were no trees to be seen for miles. And very little color. The tufts of grass were a drab brown color and the sky a somber gray. One's eyes could travel for miles across this barren landscape, and not see any sign of human life. Susannah's heart held a strange foreboding. Was this what being homesick felt like?

John said they'd arrive today. Somehow Susannah was loath to leave the train. She was tired by now of the jostling and jerking of the trip, but it was familiar at least. Once they got off and stepped into the cold

January air they'd be on Iowa soil. From what she'd seen so far, she couldn't help but wish they could just stay on the train and keep going.

From the station it would still be nearly twenty miles to the place they would call home. She could see that John was eager to be there. For a man used to hard work, the long trip with little to occupy himself was a trial. No wonder John hadn't wanted to come all the way up to Canada! Susannah allowed herself a wry little smile at the thought. Now that she'd seen what travel was like, she was all the more certain she'd made the right decision in asking him to come for her if he wanted to marry her. It had been scary enough coming out here with him, let alone traveling by herself to meet him somewhere.

She shuddered as she recalled the city of Chicago. Yesterday when they had arrived there, they needed to change from one train to another. Never had she even imagined such a hubbub of confusion! Train tracks crisscrossed each other in the railyard like a tangle of thread, with people dashing to and fro and shouting to no one in particular. Large, belching trains sat idling on sidings, and porters and personnel dashed between them as if in a race with time, carrying boxes and crates of every size. Inside the station throngs of people were jostling and crowding together. Susannah had never seen anything like it before. It had made her dizzy. She had clutched John's coat sleeve in near panic. Why, if she lost him, she was sure there'd be no way she could ever find him again.

Finally it was over. John had seen to it that their crates and boxes were transferred. He seemed undisturbed by all the confusion and clamor. When they were finally seated again, and the train began creeping through the city's miles of factories and buildings, she was relieved. The snow looked dirty and soiled. It lay in smoke-stained piles along the streets. The grime of tall buildings peered out through dirty snow at the gray winter sky. Who could live in such a place? Then she remembered: not everyone had a choice of where they lived.

Now as they neared the end of their journey, Susannah did her best to share John's eagerness. But in spite of all he'd told her about it, it was still intimidating. Not only was the surrounding countryside so much different from the Ontario she knew, there would be no human being she knew either.

Only John.

The thought hit her. But it didn't offer much comfort just now. For really, she didn't know him very well either. Then she reprimanded herself silently. God was in Iowa too. He wasn't confined to a single township in Ontario. The thought relaxed her. Just as He had been with her on life's journey so far, He would continue. But she would have to trust Him. Perhaps more than ever before.

✳   ✳

Groggily Susannah opened her eyes. Bright sunlight streamed into the room. She sat up with a start. Why was she in bed when it was daylight? Her foggy mind groped for answers.

Oh, yes. They were in Iowa now. Late last night the grueling trip had ended at last. She had been really tired before they even got off the train. Unused to travel, she had been unable to rest like she wished to. When the train pulled away from Ocheyedan, leaving them there with their parcels and crates, the final leg of their trip began. John had arranged for a team to be there to take them the remaining miles out to May City.

Now she recalled numbly climbing in, then waiting for John to load the things. It was winter, after all, so buffalo robes were piled on thickly. John urged the team time and again. He wanted badly to be there before nightfall. Snuggled deep in the robes, with her face wound by a woolen scarf, she hadn't been able to see much on the way out. But there wasn't much to see. How John knew the way was beyond her. Sameness surrounded them. Miles of it. At last, weariness had claimed her in sleep. It really hadn't been so cold—not colder than Canada. In spite of John's urgings it was dark when they arrived at his brother Emmanuel's farm. Now she recalled the awkward arrival. Curious children had clustered tightly about them, wanting to see firsthand the new bride their Uncle John had brought from back East. Susannah couldn't recall much of the rest of the evening. She'd been so weary. It had been a blessed relief to sink into this bed at last. That it was no doubt a bed sacrificed by someone else in the family now dawned on her. She wondered where John was.

He'd said they would stay here with Emmanuel's until he could get a home built on the property between here and his father's farm. It was to be on a section of his parents' farm.

A new home. Susannah pondered this. Just for them! It was more than she expected. Excitement returned, and she hastened to dress. No doubt it was an embarrassment to John that she wasn't already up. She smiled to herself. Perhaps John had asked them to let her sleep. Those few days of getting to know him on board the train had taught her that he was kind enough to do something like that.

But now it was high time she got up and did her part. Today was, after all, her first day of a new beginning here on the prairie.

chapter 26

Fitting In

Susannah was relieved when warmer weather arrived at last.
It meant she and John could move to a small outbuilding
Emmanuel owned. John was working on their own home, but progress
was slow. She couldn't help feeling like a nuisance in this home which
already had six children. The small room they used as their bedroom
belonged to the boys, who in the meantime were crowded into the attic
on makeshift mats. Besides, there was no privacy. Curious eyes always
seemed to be watching to see what this new lady from Canada would
do next.

At least there was plenty of work. Susannah was glad for this. In all
her life, work had been a staple. It was now also the only way she could
justify her existence in this busy home. Amelia's hands were more
than full with her brood. John likewise helped as he could with the
farmwork while they lived here with Emmanuel and Amelia. The work
they did took care of their room and board.

Emmanuel and Amelia had also lived in the same small outbuilding
while they built their own house. In the meantime it had been used
as storage for various things. As soon as possible, Susannah took a
broom and dustpan to the interior of the shed-like structure. Soon a

collection of cobwebs scurried out the door. She carried in their crates and arranged them in the corners. At least now all their things could be together here with them. John helped her set up a makeshift table. In one corner they placed heavy blankets to form a temporary bed. When all this was done, Susannah surveyed it in satisfaction. With one of the braided rugs upon the bare floor, it really did look homey. *It's our own little nest,* she thought whimsically.

It seemed as though she rarely saw John these days. A lumber order had been placed, as there was nothing here on the prairie to build with—unless one cut sod strips for a home. That wasn't what John had in mind. The lumber was to arrive by train. It was then loaded on large sleds and fetched by teams the last leg of its journey.

This seemed so unusual to Susannah. Where she came from, trees had to be cleared before one could farm. There was plenty of lumber to build anything one desired, all for the cutting. To order lumber by train was unheard of in Ontario! Well, this is Iowa, she reminded herself.

Once the lumber was hauled in and stacked, John seemed to relax. He had badly wanted to get it here before the prairie thawed and the roads became too muddy for such heavy loads. Now, with the frequent traffic of teams driving in and out to the building site with the supplies, the reality of their new home started to be visible. A lane of sorts appeared. Though John had showed her where it was to be, Susannah could now imagine it better.

John spent every spare hour framing the house. He often didn't come in until dark, when he could no longer see his measurements. After their simple supper there was sometimes the chance to visit before he went to bed to rest his tired body from the exhausting work.

Susannah had come to anticipate their evening talks, but sometimes John was too tired to say much. Sometimes he only spoke of how the work was going. Though it was only ordinary talk, it forged a strong bond for this couple who had barely known each other.

One evening Susannah voiced a question that had entered her mind that day. The fact that she didn't know was a keen reminder just how little she really knew about her husband.

She couldn't think of how to word it tactfully. The only way she could think of was to ask outright. When John paused in conversation, it could wait no longer.

"John," she asked curiously. "How old are you?"

He raised his head and looked at her in surprise. A sly smile curved his lips. "Well, now! I was born in 1875, so I guess I'm 25." He seemed to take his time answering, as if he hadn't considered this for a while either.

"Yes, that's right. Later this year I'll be 26. Now," he paused, "how old are you?"

Susannah blushed. "Exactly the same," she replied. "I'll be 26 this year too." Her eyes met John's and she noted the sparkle in his. She felt by the heat on her cheeks that her face was probably bright pink. It seemed as though they'd just shared a secret.

John chuckled merrily. "Now that the important things have been taken care of, do you think I should go ahead and finish the house? Two old folks like us should have their own home, don't you think?"

"Ach, you!" Susannah knew he was teasing.

One day she found courage to ask him about another matter that had niggled her mind for some time. At first she'd tried to ignore it, since it was mostly remarks made by Emmanuel's children. Susannah knew children tended to speak bluntly about what was on their mind. But lately it occurred to her that maybe she should reconsider the matter. Especially since she'd heard a similar comment from a lady in the community. It bothered her and she decided to ask John.

"Do you think I'm too fancy?" Once again she couldn't think how else to approach the subject except directly.

John absorbed the question. A few moments passed before he slowly asked, "What do you mean?"

"My coverings, for instance," she began. "The women here don't have lace on theirs. None of them. Should I take mine off my coverings?"

John looked thoughtful. "Maybe you should," he said slowly. "They do some things differently here than in the Canadian community."

Susannah nodded. She had noticed. She had also sensed an

undercurrent of something she couldn't quite put her finger on. Maybe she'd just imagined it. She had always been sensitive about fitting in, so maybe some of it was her imagination. In Canada she hadn't fit in when her clothes were plainer than others', but now the tables were turned. Here you didn't fit in if your clothes were prettier.

She was still pondering these things when John spoke again.

"We don't want to be an offense to anyone. Romans chapter 14 speaks plainly about that. If something we do offends our brethren, we shouldn't do it." After a pause he continued. "This community was started with intentions of being very conservative. Older members saw where all the liberal choices were leading, and it was a cause for concern. Even in small details they took a strong stand against pride. They believed unnecessary frills on clothes are directly related to pride."

Susannah could tell he'd given thought to his reply. It made her feel secure to have his serious opinion. She knew his answer was sound. She also had no wish to upset anyone. Even more than that, she felt the deep need to fit in and belong. Nowhere in life had she ever felt that she really belonged. Not yet. She'd hoped so much that here at last that might become reality.

Here in Iowa the landscape itself made her feel vulnerable. There were no trees for shelter from anything nature chose to unleash. It seemed to her that everything was starkly exposed to sun, wind, snow—anything. Here where she didn't really know anyone, she felt nearly as exposed as her surroundings. It seemed that she stood out, with no protection, and was exposed to the opinions of those who were at home in familiar territory. Now, with John's guidance, she resolved to do her part in fitting in.

After her discussion with John, Susannah set about making small changes to her clothing. It really wasn't so hard to remove that narrow strip of lace that edged her coverings. She wasn't so sure about her coat though. Here, the women wore a straight-cut type, instead of the more shapely style common in Canada. She felt embarrassed to ask John for money to replace it, but decided that since it would likely lead to problems, she'd do it. She was determined to stick to her resolve—not just to be plain like the others, but to obey the biblical command to live in peace and unity with other members of the church. In light of that, it really wasn't a big deal. She could make something else out of the coat later, then it wouldn't be wasted. And she would have the blessing of knowing she'd been as obedient as she knew how to be.

chapter 27

The New Home

Just as spring arrived, Emmanuel's family became very sick. They were diagnosed with the dreaded diphtheria. Swiftly a sign was hung upon the front door alerting any potential visitors or neighbors of their plight. It read:

Quarantine

Diphtheria

Notice—no person shall be permitted to enter or leave these premises except as provided by the Rules and Regulations of the State Board of Health.

Since they were in daily contact with the family, even though they slept in the small outbuilding, John and Susannah both were exposed to the sickness. There was nothing for Susannah to do except help Amelia nurse the sick children. She did it willingly, for they certainly needed care and compassion.

Inwardly she was stricken with fear that she or John might come down with the illness. It seemed to her the house couldn't be finished fast enough. The sooner they could be in it, the better.

John was a patient, methodical worker. He liked his work to be done correctly. Once the framing was done for their new home, the siding had to go on. Then began the tedious job of cutting strips of wood into laths. These strips had to be nailed to the rafters and the studding on the inside of the home. Then they were plastered. When time allowed, Emmanuel or her father-in-law, Jacob, would help John.

From the tiny building on Emmanuel's property, Susannah could look across the prairie and see the shape of their new home rise behind a gentle knoll in the field. Her heart warmed to think of all the hard work John was putting into it. Surely they would have a happy home! If he didn't get sick. The fear was never far from her mind, but she knew it was out of her control to protect him from the germs of that alarming illness. What if God led her this far, out into a land of strangers, and then let her husband become stricken?

Ach, she shook herself. It did no good to worry. Nevertheless, no one was more relieved than she once the crisis passed, leaving its victims pale and weak, but alive. Neither she nor John came down with it. For this Susannah was greatly thankful. Once more she resolved to place her full trust in the great God who had spared them from it.

At last John announced the home ready for his bride. With joy Susannah settled in. There was a kitchen and their bedroom on the first floor. A division in the center of these two rooms held the narrow stairwells that led either to the cellar or the tiny upstairs rooms under the eaves. John had carefully built neat doors to both of the stairways, so they would need to heat only the two rooms on the first floor. There was even a low attic. What luxury!

Susannah dared to dream of a future when they might actually need the space of those two rooms upstairs. In the meantime, she carefully arranged her few possessions where she decided they would fit best. Their clothes were hung neatly from pegs in their bedroom. John spoke of someday adding a summer kitchen to the side of the house, but for now it already seemed like a palace. And all her own! She couldn't get used to the idea that she no longer needed to do things the way other women wanted them done. That realization was foreign to her.

Now that the house was done, John was free to begin farming. The days had lengthened and the sunlight strengthened. Spring thaws followed by rain had left mud in unbelievable amounts. It could hardly be removed from one's boots and shoes. Susannah found the weight of it tagging along with every step depressing.

Warm sunshine and the ever-present wind finally won out. Faint tints of green were visible across the rolling swells. This merged into a solid carpet of ever-deepening green. Grasses danced and swayed, whispering greetings to all who had survived the harsh winter. As the days became warmer and longer, bright colors budded and bloomed among the grass.

There was even a startling splash of brilliant red. Emmanuel's children taught Susannah as many names of the wildflowers as they knew. Those crimson ones she so enjoyed were called Indian Paintbrush. There were large pink daisy shapes whose petals hung down away from a dark center. Those were coneflowers. There were white daisies with centers as bright as new butter, as well as black-eyed-Susans. There were also dainty blues and purples lurking shyly among the green grasses for which Susannah had no names.

In midsummer the wild roses bloomed. Their soft pink blossoms charmed Susannah. Their five simple petals were crowned in the center with a delicate circlet of dainty, hairlike, yellow stems. No matter if they were thorny, Susannah loved them. She gathered a large bunch one day to grace her simple kitchen with their beauty.

Before Susannah could have believed it, a year had flown by. Her first winter in Iowa was over. It had been severe, but they had survived. John, having lived there longer, knew it was wise to build one's home in the lowest part of the property, so it wouldn't catch all the wind. Even so, it seemed the wind beat relentlessly upon their new home. There was a bit too much truth to John's joke that you never need to hang up your hat outdoors. You could just lay it up alongside the wall of the barn, and the wind kept it plastered firmly in place.

The rows of cottonwoods they'd planted in the fall for a windbreak were no help yet. Sometimes it snowed so hard one could see nothing. Other times it might not be snowing at all, but the wind picked up snow from the ground and hurled it into the air in a mock blizzard.

But now spring was coming again, Susannah couldn't help but travel back to Ontario in her memory. It would be maple sugar time there. That was a job she'd always enjoyed. She sighed. It was no use wishing for what one didn't have. Besides, there was plenty to do here.

In early April of 1902, Emmanuel and Amelia had another son, Norman. Susannah welcomed the chance to cross the field and help care for him.

By the 30th of May, it was their turn. John and Susannah became parents to a tiny Mary. With a full heart Susannah chose the name of her own mother. While she could hardly fathom that this was her own child, she delighted in caring for her. The responsibility hung heavy as well. Though only a tiny bundle, the baby had a never-dying soul. Could they teach her and train her so she could become one of God's children? This was Susannah's prayer.

As never before, Susannah faced her own painful life, devoid of any real love or protection. She shuddered. Even John didn't understand her almost fierce desire to protect her baby from the hard and cruel things in life. But then, he'd been brought up in a family that stuck together and cared for each other.

Since coming to Iowa, Susannah had come to know John's parents better. It wasn't long before she realized John had inherited his mother's good-natured kindness. Nancy Anna, known as Mother Brubaker to the family, was the same lady whose kindness long ago in Canada to Susannah's sister had even then won her a warm spot in Susannah's heart. Since she had never known the stability of a mother's love and steadfast example, Mother Brubaker now filled some of that void.

Even as she absorbed that motherly woman's ideals, there remained a deep-seated inferiority in Susannah. She couldn't put it into words. Being around other families, and especially other women, made her feel that she was somehow less than they. The inner struggle with this made her likely to keep to the edge of any gathering. Memories of being reprimanded for nearly everything she did surfaced without her permission. Feeling as though others must be able to see at a glance when she didn't get everything done perfectly caused her to raise a subconscious barrier of defense.

Not long after moving to Iowa, Susannah realized there was tension in the group of Mennonites there. Families who had moved in from Indiana and Pennsylvania were used to strict rules, while the members from Canada had more lenient views and practices. To complicate matters, the entire ministry, including Bishop Jesse Bauman, were all former Canadians.

The brethren from Ontario continued to wear beards as they had back home, while those from other areas did not. Since the bishop was bearded, he gave the others freedom to choose as their conscience directed. The result was that about half of the men wore facial hair. The ones who chose not to felt there needed to be more unity in the matter.

Soon another matter arose that divided the opinions of church members. While Bishop Bauman was away on one of his many travels, a lady in the community lay very ill. Fearing she was near death's door, and not being a baptized believer, she implored Minister Amos Bauman to baptize her lest she die before the bishop's return.

Amos hesitated. Here was a dilemma. The bishop was the only one authorized to perform believers' baptism to those who expressed the desire to be a part of the Lord's body.

But with the bishop absent, and the woman and her family beseeching him to administer the rite, Amos relented. He helped the woman understand her need of repentance and God's forgiveness, then baptized her.

This upset some members of the community. When Jesse returned, he was speedily made aware of the incident. A decision was made to silence Amos because he had performed the deed.

Susannah thought this unfair. Her own past made her keenly aware of injustice. John and she agreed that Amos had only done what any conscientious minister of the gospel should have done. Besides, the lady recovered from her serious illness. Could that not be an indication that the baptism had been sanctioned by God?

Not all felt this way. There was much talk, and Susannah occasionally voiced her feelings to other women in the neighborhood. If she had imagined herself the object of talk before, now it was real. She was quickly blamed for speaking out of turn.

Some reproached her outspokenness with the added blame that she was just "one of Indian John Heckendorn's daughters."

"Never been taught much, that family."

"Always knew how things should be done, John did. But couldn't manage his own household."

Remarks like this stung Susannah to the core.

"Don't let it bother you," John comforted his wife. "People talk too much."

But it did bother Susannah. It bothered her deeply to see someone treated wrongly.

Neither she nor John were surprised to learn a year later that Amos and Lydia Bauman were planning to move from the community.

In April of 1903 an ordination for another minister was held. The lot fell on Elam Martin, a young man only in his twenties. Susannah felt sorry for his petite wife, Lovina. The neighborhood had just experienced a painful episode. What could the couple expect of their new position of service in the community?

She resolved afresh to support them and give them no cause for grief on her part. Susannah knew John felt the same way.

chapter 28

Learning to Be Thankful

June of 1904 came around. On the fourteenth of the month another daughter came to bless John and Susannah. They named her Magdalena.

It seemed very fitting to Susannah that in this season of fresh, new growth all about the farm and across the prairie, there was also a new little baby in the house. A fresh little soul sent to them from heaven above. The immensity of their responsibility to guide that same soul back to her Maker lay heavily upon Susannah's heart. If she thought about it too long, it nearly took away the joy of caring for the infant.

It was much easier to take care of her children's needs materially than to have to worry about their eternal needs. But even that was a day by day work. John proved to be a good, kind husband and provided well.

There was always plenty to eat, though not always the variety of food that Susannah had been used to in Ontario. She was grateful for Betsy's teachings on "making do" with what was at hand. It warmed her heart that the crops had likewise done well so far, and John's small herd of animals could be fed and comfortably kept.

The prairie, though rolling in appearance, did not drain well. When it rained heavily every small lake and even sloughs and creeks filled with water and turned into temporary ponds. When this happened the fish that lived in normal bodies of water explored their enlarged new boundaries. This was fun for them until the water receded, leaving fish galore trapped in low-lying puddles. In a short time one could easily harvest a wagon load of fish left behind as they faced certain death from lack of oxygen. Even with lots gathered, there were plenty left dying on the mud for the seagulls to feast upon.

In many ways Susannah was getting used to living on the prairie, but there was still one thing she couldn't rein in her fear of—tornadoes. John's stories about tornadoes chilled Susannah to the center of her being. The winds during a tornado could be so wild and strong that whole houses were blown away. Since no trees were there to block the wind, one might as well expect that any structure in its path would be picked up and tossed about like a child's plaything. Also, they were so unpredictable. Perhaps that was the worst part. You never knew when one of the howling monsters would appear. The sultry days of early summer seemed to spawn the tornadoes. Now that Susannah had two small dependent daughters to take care of, she dreaded that season even more.

John had wisely built a nice cellar under their home. If time allowed, she knew that this was where she and the girls must go to wait out the roar of those awful winds. She eyed the slender forms of the trees John had planted in five neat rows. In time they might provide a sheltering windbreak for their house and barn. They had survived the elements so far, but they weren't large enough or strong enough to provide security yet. Susannah longed for the stately forms of the maples and pines back in Ontario. Oh, to live in a place where no such things as these dreaded tornadoes existed!

John often lamented the absence of fruit. Many times he expressed the desire to his wife to be able to grow crunchy, delicious apples here in Iowa. Susannah did her best to prepare puddings made from the tart wild plums that grew along the creek during their season. If only one could stretch that season into winter! The mulberries yielded juicy berries, but with two small ones to care for she nearly always lost those sweet juicy fruits to her winged competitors.

No one could lament the lush stands of corn that sprang from the dark Iowa soil though. It was especially pleasing to John, following his hard work to break up the tough prairie sod into tillable fields, to see those young blades of green pop up from their dark bed. Day by day they seemingly stretched up toward the sky as though propelled from beneath by an unseen force. As summer progressed, the ears on the corn matured into fat, golden cobs. Susannah sensed John's joy as he inspected the crop. Though modest, he remarked one evening towards fall, "Looks like there'll be plenty of cornbread for my girls to eat this winter!" The happy twinkle in his eye warmed Susannah's heart.

"And plenty of cobs to burn in the stove," she added.

"Yes! Let the blizzards come. The Lord has provided well for us, hasn't He, Susannah?"

She nodded. This was so like her John. Even though wheat didn't flourish here, corn did, so they would just eat cornbread instead of wheat bread. Since there was no wood to burn in the stove, corncobs were gathered diligently to feed into the hungry maw of their black stove. If one tamped them in tightly enough, they burned slowly and provided welcome warmth from the blustery winter air. It had taken her nearly all of the previous winter to learn how to manage the heat consistently enough to prepare meals.

As John had so truthfully pointed out just now, the Lord had provided for them. Yes, He had. Susannah could see it well. The provisions were different from what she was used to and she had to trust God in a way she had never trusted Him before. But maybe that was good for her.

Unbidden, her thoughts turned to the children of Israel. Some of them hadn't been pleased about their journey into the wilderness, and they longed for the comforts they had back in Egypt. Never mind that there had been great hardships there too. They complained about their bleak trek through strange territory. They worried about the lack of bread, so God sent the mysterious manna to them which appeared every morning as fresh as the dew upon the grass. They accepted it grudgingly, and still grumbled that they had no meat. Surely one needed meat to survive the grueling trip they were making. Then God sent quail, thousands of quail. Well, at least it was meat, but not like the lamb and beef they were used to and craved. And Moses…was he really qualified to be their leader? Wasn't he just…one of them? He was certainly nothing out of the ordinary. And such notions as he had! Why, no wonder some in the group resented him.

The parallels in her own life startled her. Was there really so little difference in her life here in Iowa? Was she too so caught up in longing for familiar things and food that she couldn't appreciate the blessings they had here.

Dusk crept into her home on silent shadows. Susannah shivered. Why, she was no better than the Israelites of old! She saw that she needed to renew her efforts in the quest for faith and peace. It was a humbling thought. Her mind flew to John. He seemed to find it easier than she did. Perhaps it was because Iowa had been his home for more years.

Or was it because his faith was stronger than hers. Then another thought came. Maybe it was because he *chose* to be thankful from the bottom of his heart for what they *did* have.

chapter 29

Unrest

In March of 1906 another daughter joined John and Susannah's family. Susannah wished to name her Amanda, in remembrance of her brother Moses' wife. John agreed. Mary, their oldest, was overjoyed with a new baby in the home.

By now it was evident that the community had problems in the midst of their peaceful lifestyle. Rather than stay and try to regain the unity that seemed so sadly missing, some were choosing to move away from the area. One of these was Absalom Tharp, who sold his farm and moved his family back to Pennsylvania from where they had come. It was no surprise. Iowa hadn't been very kind to Absalom Tharp. His wife got sick, died, and was buried in the prairie cemetery, alongside two small sons. No one could blame Absalom for wanting to start over where there weren't so many painful memories.

Susannah longed to clutch her daughters close and keep them safe from all harm. But nowhere, she knew, was life free of troubles. It certainly hadn't been in Canada. And now, what was one to do? John was the peacemaking sort and didn't become involved in trouble easily.

It seemed Bishop Jesse Bauman no longer held the respect of his church members. There were perhaps several reasons for this, although one could hardly lay a finger on any reason why this was true. Bishop Bauman had the gift of excellent management, no one doubted that. His farm flourished. So did his cattle. He had the wisdom to know what to ship, and when, in order to receive the highest prices. His crops yielded abundantly. With seeming ease, he assisted his sons in buying farms and these likewise flourished. He was quite able to purchase new equipment with which to perform his farmwork efficiently. Perhaps because he could easily afford to buy them, it became noticeable that he no longer opposed the modern conveniences that were becoming readily available.

John advised Susannah in their private discussions that it would be best if people didn't talk so much. He himself didn't see eye to eye with some of the bishop's decisions. But he reminded his wife that Jesse was ordained as their leader, and his position was one in which God had placed him. For that reason they needed to practice respect and obedience.

Susannah agreed with this. She resolved not to become disturbed by the talk that circulated freely within the community. It was easier said than done, but as a woman there really wasn't anything she could do to change the situation. Menfolk made the major decisions. It was a wife's duty to be in submission to her husband's leadership, and for now, Susannah was glad. She could pray, and also, there was plenty of work to do, for their family was growing.

In late May of 1908 a fourth child entered their home. John was overjoyed that it was a son. He wanted to name the baby Enoch. Susannah too rejoiced over their son. Now maybe in years to come John would have someone to help him with the year-round farmwork.

That is, if the Lord willed, and the infant remained healthy. Just this year there had been a serious bout with scarlet fever in the area. Numerous families had been quarantined.

A community custom was for families to visit in homes where there was a new baby. "I do hope no one brings us the scarlet fever germ," Susannah mused aloud, voicing her concern. She had been so careful to stay home and away from such dreaded sicknesses before the baby arrived.

"Maybe with winter behind us, the sickness will slacken off," John said.

Susannah knew he shared her concern. But with summer upon them there was no time to worry. Work needed to be done from sunup to sundown.

Once the land was worked and the crops planted there was a lull until harvest came. John's worries weren't only for the family, but for his crop. The corn was nearing two feet tall, marching in long straight rows across his fields of black soil, when a late frost covered the prairie.

Susannah had never seen her husband so dejected. And for good reason. The corn was the major food supply for the family and animals. Not only that, but the cobs heated their home during the winter. What would they do? One could easily see that the frost had completely killed the plants, and it was too late to plant another crop this year.

"We'll have to make do some way," John stated tonelessly, hardly meeting Susannah's gaze.

"How? With what?" she asked.

He shook his head wordlessly. The look on his face invited no further questions.

We can hope and pray for a mild winter then, Susannah thought. *That's the only way we'll make it.*

It wasn't to be. Fall came early, with winter right on its heels. John did his best to prepare for the family. Other community men did likewise. Dried cow dung was gathered from barnyards and pastures. This was piled up to burn in the stove. Men mowed the tough bluestem grass in every slough and buffalo wallow they could find. These were twisted and dried, also to burn in stoves.

The first snow fell early. It was driven by the wind, seeking for any crack and crevice to enter. John took a long rope and nailed it to the corner of the house. Grimly he stretched it out toward the barn and fastened the other end to the side of the barn, close to the door. This was to hold on to should the blizzard become severe. There was too much truth in stories of people getting lost in the blinding snow, even in such a short distance.

When he entered the house after doing the chores, a puff of snow came in with him, scattering quickly across the floor.

Last summer John had built a lean-to kitchen to their home. Susannah was grateful for the extra space with their growing family. Now, to save heat, the door leading to it was firmly closed, and so was the upstairs door. The children would be bedded down close to the stove. Any warmth coming from it wouldn't reach far in such a howling storm as this one.

chapter 30

Blizzard

"Shall I tell you a story, children?" John asked.

"Yes! Yes!" came the girls' answer. Story time with their father was always special. Tonight, with the roaring wind outdoors it would be a welcome diversion.

"Which story would you like?" asked John.

"Indian story!" came Magdalena's request.

"No, tell about the whistling well!" This came from Mary, the oldest.

"Yes, the well story!" chimed in Amanda.

"All right. Tell the well story," agreed Magdalena.

John pulled a chair close to the stove and was instantly flanked by the three girls, eagerly crowding close.

Susannah, having done her chores, and feeling her own need of a distraction from worries caused by the fierce blizzard outside, decided to join the circle. Grabbing Enoch, who was bundled as tightly as possible, Susannah pulled him close and cherished the warmth of his small body.

John began his story with a wink in Susannah's direction. She smiled in return. These stories were fun for her too. It was about her husband before she'd met him. "When I was a boy we decided to have a well dug on Daudy Brubaker's farm," John said. "The well driller came out one Saturday from Ocheyedan with his rig. He drilled and drilled until it was about 300 feet deep. Then he wanted to pull the drill out to put down more casing. Suddenly there was lots of noise! Even more than the noisy drill. As soon as the drill was out of the deep hole, there came a blast of air from deep down in the well, way down deep. Sand, gravel, and stones shot up. A wind from deep inside the earth blew the dirt and gravel straight up, nearly 60 feet into the air!"

"Higher than our house?" asked Mary incredulously.

"Yes, higher than that," John replied to his astonished audience.

"Then what?" asked Amanda.

"Mr. Boyd, the well driller, decided we should try to cover the hole of the well. We hunted for a large rock to cover it with, but that made no difference… The power of the air coming up lifted the rock right off again. A board was placed on it, with a man seated on top. That wasn't heavy enough either. The pressure pushed them away too."

"What was it?" Magdalena's girlish mind couldn't grasp this.

"We don't know for sure," John said slowly. "No one had ever seen anything like it. Not even the well driller. And not even the newspapermen from town."

"Was it in the newspaper?" asked Mary.

"Yes," said John. "Lots of people heard about it and came to see if it was true. And because it was such a strange event, there was even an article in the newspaper."

"Could people hear it?" asked Mary.

"Some people could." John chuckled at the memory. "Especially once we put a steam whistle on it. Then the blast could be heard from miles away, all across the neighborhood!"

"How long did it do that?" The girls had plenty of questions, even though they'd heard the story before.

"About seven hours straight," John answered. "Then it slowed down a bit. But off and on for the next few days it blew again, with gravel flying way up into the air. Once when it slowed down, we cut a wooden plug to fit down into the pipe, thinking we could stop it off, since there wasn't any water in it anyway."

"Did that stop it then?"

"Until the next blast of air came. Then it blew the plug way up into the sky."

"What made it do that? What was it?" The girls' eyes were wide in their amazement.

"We decided the well went into some sort of air cave, instead of reaching water," John said. "No one knew for sure. Someone from the newspaper had heard of such wells up north in the Dakotas. But around here it was unheard of. It is one of those things that God created that we people don't understand."

"I'm glad our well didn't do that," Mary said soberly. "That would have scared me." Her two sisters nodded in agreement. Susannah shared their thankfulness.

The wind shrieking around the corner of their home was scary enough. She eyed the pile of twisted straw in the corner of the kitchen. Would there be enough? Would the blizzard abate before their meager supply ran out?

John rose from his chair and acted out the thoughts of his wife. He lifted the stove lid to feed another bundle of dried bluestem onto the hungry red coals.

"Bedtime now, don't you think?" he said calmly to the girls.

Magdalena shuddered. "I think I hear a whistling well right now," she commented.

John chuckled. "That's the wind you hear. It's a blizzard. You know what that is."

"Will our house blow away?" Amanda asked fearfully.

"We'll ask God to keep that from happening," John said firmly. When the family was all bedded down, the girls on makeshift blankets on the floor close to the stove and the baby with herself and John in their bed, Susannah could still hear the wind moan. Sometimes the whole house shook. She recalled John's assurance to their daughters that they would ask God to protect them. She'd already done so. But now, her body tense from all the turbulence about them, she did so again.

It was a restless night. The twisted grass didn't hold heat long at all, and John frequently rose to stuff another hunk into the stove.

By morning the blizzard still raged. John opened the door once to peer into the dim whirl of whiteness. Large chunks of snow fell into the room. The barn was invisible. Wordlessly John went for the shovel kept in the lean-to kitchen. The animals had to be cared for, regardless of the storm.

Wrapping another scarf around his neck and face, he disappeared into the whiteness.

"Keep hold of the rope, John!" Susannah urged her husband. There was no need to explain the warning.

It seemed hours to her until John returned. She knew he would have to shovel alongside the rope, so could even reach the barn.

When he finally returned she was nearly as anxious as the children. Quickly she pulled up a chair and helped remove his frozen mittens and scarf. The snow which fell from his wraps landed in piles on the floor, not in any hurry to melt. There was lots of frozen snow and moisture in John's dark beard. A woolen scarf was no match for blizzard-driven snow.

Susannah was relieved to have John safely back in the house. Surely today the fury would subside. For now he was safely beside the warmth of the stove, and there would be no more work outside for the rest of the day.

Later, Susannah could not say how they had survived the three-day storm. She did know her nerves were nearly spent. When the wind finally abated and left a strange quietness in the void of its angry roar, she could hardly find words with which to thank the Lord for sparing her family and their home.

chapter 31

A Welcome Spring

At least there were potatoes with which to feed her family. Susannah couldn't imagine how else they'd have survived the long winter. Amelia had taught them how to slice and bake them on top of the stove. With a pat of butter and a dash of salt, the children ate them willingly, especially if they were baked until nearly crisp. John preferred soup made with them, and since they went further that way, that was usually what she did.

What would I do without Amelia close by? Susannah wondered many a time. Now that she was raising a family, many times Susannah relied on her sister-in-law's greater experience in child rearing. The cousins close by provided playmates and diversions from the oftentimes tiresome sameness of day by day life here on the vast, open prairie.

One of Emmanuel's older sons, discouraged by the lack of trees on their farm, had brought home a few acorns from a trip back East. The lad lavished his acorns with nearly as much care as one might a prized calf or piglet. He was rewarded by two sprouts, then saplings. These he planted with great care close to their home.

Susannah joined the youngster in disappointment when one of the horses nibbled off one of the saplings. The other sapling, however, thrived, and Susannah enjoyed watching the slow progress of that slender young oak. Would it ever mature into a mighty tree the likes of which she'd been used to in Ontario? Though the cottonwood grove John had planted as a windbreak was growing fast, she often missed the stately hardwoods of back home.

Gradually, so gradually that at first one hardly dared believe it, the brutal winter slackened in strength. Everyone rejoiced when the weather finally became mild enough that the children could play outdoors again.

John, whose hopes were renewed by the return of spring, was eager to return to his beloved farming. The soil was hardly dry enough when he took the team out to start plowing for this year's crop.

Susannah began to air the home for spring on the day John began plowing. With the children outside playing, this was her chance. She paused a moment to watch John's plow turn over a nearly black furrow of soil in the nearby field. *Won't be long until the gulls spot him,* she thought to herself.

A short time later she heard panic-stricken cries coming from Amanda, playing in the grove of trees. Quickly she grabbed little Enoch and headed outside to see what the danger was.

From here she could see the four-year-old on the swing John had hung from the tallest branch of a young tree. John had heard the frantic calls as well. He stopped the team at the front end of the field and sprinted toward them. He reached their daughter before Susannah did.

Panting to catch her breath, Susannah heard John ask Amanda, "What's wrong?"

"I'm scared!" the girl sobbed, not loosening her white-knuckled grip on the ropes of the swing.

"Of what?" John asked patiently.

"That noise! What is it?" wailed Amanda.

John looked at his wife, expecting her to know, but Susannah was as puzzled as he was.

Finally Amanda pointed to the flock of screeching gulls circling the freshly plowed field. "Those things!" she said on a sob-laden breath.

"What are they? They make so much noise, and they're chasing you, Dad! I was afraid to go off the swing and run. I was sure they're going to chase me too!"

Bravely John stifled a guffaw. "They're not chasing me. They just want every fat worm the plow turns over," he explained. "They're hungry after the long winter. See, they're just screeching because they're happy. They won't chase you, Amanda."

Susannah glanced at her husband, thankful that he hadn't laughed at the childish fear, though she was also tempted to chuckle. "Do you want to come in with me now?" she invited.

With a swift nod Amanda scooted off the seat of the swing.

Susannah knew she would have to find something else for the lively youngster to do soon. The two older girls were occupied with garden work. This left the younger Amanda at loose ends. After a short unsuccessful attempt at entertaining Enoch, Susannah welcomed the next diversion.

Mattie, the children's cousin, appeared at their door, a covered bucket in one hand and a large stick in the other.

"Come in," Susannah greeted the lass. "What can we get for you today?"

"Mother sent me over to see if someone can go with me down to the creek for frogs," came Mattie's answer. "We don't have any other meat right now."

"Mary and Magdalena are busy," Susannah replied, "but Amanda could go with you. We'd use our share of frogs for our own supper too."

Arming Amanda with the milk pail and a lid, she sent the two on their way. A creek ran through a corner of the pasture. In early summer the marshy banks were heavily populated with frogs. A good panful of frog legs would be a welcome springtime treat. That is, if the girls were successful in their hunt.

Susannah paused to watch from the window. From here she could see the two down by the creek. She could see their stealthy advances, the raised arms, and the swift whop of the stick, but she couldn't see how many of the whops resulted in an actual frog for the bucket.

With an almost envious sigh she left the window and returned to her own work. After the long winter, such a lovely day made it hard to remain inside. But it was her duty to care for and provide for the comfort of her family. And really, with such a balmy breeze coming in the window, it wasn't such a punishment.

An hour later she heard voices nearing the house. This told her the girls were returning from their hunt. A glance in that direction told her the contents of the bucket consisted of some weight.

Mattie paused to wait while the younger Amanda rested her arm. When they reached the house, both came panting into the kitchen.

Seeing their flushed faces, Susannah urged them to get a drink of water from the pail and dipper in the corner.

"Did you get enough for supper?" she asked.

Mattie nodded. "Both buckets are full," she said. "But Amanda couldn't hit very well. I got most of them."

"Well, then you must take most of them home," Susannah replied. "There are more in your family anyhow."

Mattie looked pleased. "I must take them home right away. Mother wants them for supper."

"I must clean these too. John likes frog legs. Thank you, Mattie," Susannah said. She helped the girls divide the slippery spoils, making sure to keep only enough to feed her family.

Mattie hefted her heaping bucket and set off in the direction of home.

This time Amanda was able to keep Enoch occupied. Susannah was grateful. The task of cleaning the frog legs took all her concentration. Finally she tossed the last one into the bowl. Swishing a dipper of water over them, she rinsed them thoroughly.

When John came in at dusk, a delicious aroma met his nose. He sniffed appreciatively and quickly washed up from his day's work.

The girls did likewise. After their customary offer of thanksgiving for the food before them, the family dug in.

Young Amanda took a generous helping. Susannah smiled. Maybe the lass had missed quite a few with her aim this afternoon, but now that they were fried in butter, she apparently didn't intend to miss them again.

chapter 32

Problems

Community life was becoming increasingly unsettling. Strong currents of suspicion undermined the brotherly goodwill sought so earnestly by the first Mennonites in the settlement.

The ministry, which some have likened to a protective grove of trees planted as a shelter around a set of buildings, could no longer maintain a structured harbor for its members. No longer did the members of the May City community feel protected from the fierce blasts of worldly influences. Instead, they sensed gaps in the leadership, through which raw elements of changing winds seeped into their lives and undermined their respect for Bishop Bauman.

Jesse Bauman, an easygoing man by nature, found it hard to resist the tide of drift. His affluence made it possible to purchase equipment to make his own lifestyle much easier. His cattle continued to flourish. On long drives to herd cattle to the railyards, he was away from home for extended lengths of time. A common courtesy for cattlemen outside the Mennonite circle was to take turns purchasing strong drinks for all those involved in the grueling work of herding and loading the cattle. Bishop Bauman, not wishing to be rude, as his were often a large portion of the herds, also took his turn in supplying drinks. Rumor now had it that he had begun to indulge in such drinks himself.

Here was a dilemma. The Mennonite settlers, accustomed to harsh blizzards and sub-zero winter weather, knew well how easily a person could freeze to death in over-exposure in their brutal climate. Thus, the use of whiskey was not entirely forbidden in the community. Many times a swig of it was the only way for a man out in the elements to keep warm. It was also used as medicine. The settlers were often miles away from town and any doctor, so a bottle of such spirits was kept in nearly every home. It was used to fight off coughing which could so easily turn into deadly pneumonia.

On the other hand, the scriptural principles deeply embedded in their hearts and minds forbade indulgence in the tonic, knowing it could quickly become an addiction. What could they do now? To bring an accusation against their bishop, should it be ungrounded, was also a sin (I Timothy 5:19).

The bishop's sons and daughters were intermarried into family circles throughout the community. How could he be remonstrated without causing a lot of hurt feelings and resentment? Attempts were made to reason with the bishop, but were met with indifference.

John, ever patient and longsuffering, continued to hope that with enough forbearance Bishop Bauman would see the error of his ways and change.

Susannah could see that it bothered him more than he admitted. She suspected this was why John poured himself into farmwork like never before. Always a hard worker, he now put in even longer days in his fields. Though he never voiced it in so many words, Susannah sensed that he felt the futility of the situation keenly.

As the days lengthened into summer, the heat unfurling across the prairie became nearly as oppressive as the previous winter's icy blasts.

"Mother," said Magdalena one day, "Father is resting out by the cornfield with his hat over his face. He didn't even want a drink. Is he sick?"

Susannah drew in a sharp breath. Last night she had noticed that John looked pale under his summer tan.

Now she hurried her steps toward the cornfield. The haying was done, but John was attempting to cultivate the lush corn stand once more. Had he been overcome by the unseasonal heat, or was he simply taking a much-needed break? Her heart nearly in her throat, Susannah turned the corner of the last row. Then she spotted him, sprawled in the shade of the waist-high corn.

"John!" she called as she neared. "Is something wrong?"

With relief she saw him stir. By now she had reached his side. She bent over him. "What's wrong?" she asked breathlessly.

"I'm very dizzy," he said slowly.

"Can you sit up?" she asked.

He nodded, and did so.

Susannah helped him to his feet, anxiously watching as he swayed unsteadily.

"You are sick," she stated bluntly.

"Not really. Just tired. And dizzy," came his answer.

"Come in and rest," she urged. "This heat isn't good. I'll help you. The girls can drive the team up to the barn."

Never had the walk from the field to the house seemed so long. Several times John staggered dizzily even with her steadying arm.

Finally they made it. Susannah quickly fetched a dipper of water from the pail in the corner. John took only a shallow swallow. Seeing this, alarm rose in Susannah's breast. Soaking a clean cloth in more water, she sponged his pale face. At her urging he agreed to lie on their bed and rest.

She hastened to the window to see how the girls were faring with the team. Heat waves shimmered along the lane leading to the barn. It looked as if all was well. The horses minded the heat as well, and plodded obediently to the barn, giving their young mistresses no trouble.

When they came in, their eyes widened upon learning that their father was resting in bed. This was unusual, and must mean he was indeed sick.

"Take Enoch and go play outside," Susannah urged. Seeing their surprise, she added, "It's too hot to do any more work today."

At this their worried faces brightened.

"Should I fetch someone from Emmanuel's?" asked Mary soberly.

"No, not yet. Let him rest a while. Then we'll see," Susannah decided.

The children left to go play in the shade of the young grove. Susannah turned back for another look at John.

His face remained unnaturally pale in the shadows of their bedroom. She could see his chest rising and falling slowly. Should she have sent for someone at Emmanuel's? How did one treat a man overcome with heat? Or was it something else? How she wished she knew!

Gently she wiped his brow once more with the damp cloth. His skin felt clammy to her touch.

"Do you want something to eat?" she asked hopefully.

"No. My stomach is already churning. Just let me rest," he said.

With that, Susannah left the room. Soon it would be choretime. She determined that John should rest and not do his evening work. But that meant she and the children would have to do it all. Was she up to it?

There was no time to think of herself. A short while later found her and the two oldest in the barn armed with milk pails.

"Now, Amanda, you must watch Enoch closely," she warned her youngest daughter. "Don't let him crawl into the pigpen."

Cautiously sitting down on the low milking stool, Susannah began the rhythm of milking the first cow. Giving the girls instructions on feeding the horses and hogs, she relaxed a bit.

Surely after a rest John will feel better, Susannah thought to herself. No doubt by morning he would want to do the milking himself.

Later, back in the house, she doubted this likelihood. John had refused supper. Silently she and the children ate their own.

At bedtime she wiped his face once more, then also his arms. His skin felt warm, nearly hot to her fingers. Oh, if only a small breeze would find its way into their small room.

Once the children were all settled for the night, Susannah had time to do what she'd longed to do ever since she'd found her husband lying out by the cornfield—take her worry to the Lord in prayer.

Quietly she knelt by their bedside. At first no words formed in her anxious mind, but once they began, Susannah poured out her situation to the One who had heard and answered so many of her pleas in the past. Knowing God had sent answers to her in wondrous ways before gave her confidence to approach Him now with concern for John. That God also sometimes chooses not to grant healing and restoration of body, she was well aware of too. For this reason she closed her plea with a tremulous, "Thy will be done, Lord."

Stiffly she arose to her feet. Then another thought popped into her mind.

"Help me to accept whatever You do, Lord," she prayed. For by now she knew that the biggest part of having peace was humbly accepting whatever the Lord chooses to send.

chapter 33

Pneumonia

After a fitful night of attempted sleep, Susannah roused herself wearily to do the morning chores again. John hadn't slept much either; rather, he'd tossed and turned, sometimes muttering incoherently.

Susannah awakened the girls to help with the milking. They responded with surprising willingness. Or was it fear of their father's condition? Susannah didn't know, but herded them toward the barn, carrying the milking pails in one hand.

The morning air was already stuffy, and promised to increase in heat as the day progressed. Susannah prayed as she sat by the cow's flanks, aiming the frothy streams into the bucket at her feet. She sought strength from above, not only for the heat-exhausted John, but for herself, to be able to carry on with the daily work.

Throughout the day, John didn't show any signs of worsening, but he was also no better.

Susannah was greatly relieved to have Emmanuel send over a son to see if John had gotten done with cultivating. Upon learning of the situation, two other sons were dispatched to finish the task for their Uncle John.

From her kitchen she couldn't see which ones they were, but she could see a team out in the cornfield. Her heart warmed at the sight. How good it was to have good neighbors! And what a blessing to have the job done, and that burden removed from her husband's mind. Gratefully she breathed a prayer of thanksgiving for this, even as she also pleaded for John's recovery.

It was a slow process. The heat stroke, for this is what they believed John's condition to be, left him weak the rest of the summer. Though grateful for help from Emmanuel's family and others in the brotherhood, both John and Susannah found it difficult to accept ongoing assistance into the harvest and threshing time.

Fall brought blessed relief from the summer's heat. But it was a brief respite. All too soon winter's blasts would be upon them again.

On December 1 another son entered their family circle. They named him Joseph. Susannah was glad Enoch had a brother now. So was John. With two sons in tow, farmwork should prosper, if they lived and were granted growth.

But before they could be of help, babies created more work. Little Joseph was no exception. Susannah was grateful for Mary and Magdalena. Both were by now quite good at being maids for her in doing little jobs. Even Amanda could do her part by watching busy little Enoch.

Susannah still tried to care for her recently ill husband. John's strength wasn't returning as he wished. The ginger tonic she prepared for him helped little. Now that the winter was here with raw blasts of cold air, she worried even more about him. She decided that to give him added energy she would make eggs for his breakfast in the morning.

Wintertime eggs were scarce, and brought in needed extra money or trade value for other staples they needed. But John needed every bit of additional strength he could get.

"We want eggs too," the children stated the first morning when she set the bowl beside John's plate.

Susannah had steeled herself for this. With a quick glance at John's face, she was afraid he would yield. For what kind of father can sit in front of his children eating special rations they coveted?

"The eggs are for Father," Susannah said, not liking the snappy way her words sounded as they hung above the breakfast table. "He needs to regain his strength. We will let him have the eggs. The rest of us will eat oatmeal." This last she attempted to add in a softer tone, though still firm enough that the children wouldn't continue to beg for eggs.

The children said no more about it, to her relief. John ate the fried eggs in silence. Susannah wanted every bite he ate to generate strength into his sparse frame.

Her fears weren't ungrounded.

One day John came in early from husking corn. His teeth were chattering in spite of being dressed warmly. His face pale, he pulled a chair up to the stove and sank into it. With closed eyes, he looked miserable.

Wordlessly Susannah felt his forehead. With alarm she noted the warmth of his skin, even though he shivered.

"You are sick," she stated flatly.

John didn't deny it.

✳   ✳

"It's pneumonia," the doctor stated.

Susannah had feared as much.

"And in the shape he's in, I just don't know…" The sentence trailed morbidly into nothing. "I'll leave a bottle of medicine. Give it to him twice a day. And keep putting that plaster on his chest."

"What else can I do for him?" Susannah asked.

The doctor only shook his head. "If the weather permits, I'll stop by again later in the week—unless there's no need to. Let me know."

Susannah knew what he meant by the mention of not being needed later in the week. While the doctor packed his bag and put on his heavy overcoat, finally wrapping his face in a woolen muffler, she fought the mental image of those words.

In a daze, she thanked him for coming. He stepped out the door and vaguely she noticed the outline of his tall form as he entered the snowy outdoors.

The chill of fear gnawed at her mind. With an involuntary shudder she lifted the stove lid and added more cobs. She must keep the house as warm as she could.

Then she slipped into the bedroom just beyond the wall. Seeing her husband so sick was something she couldn't get used to. John was the strong one. He had always been. Now here he lay, at the mercy of a siege of deadly pneumonia. Would his weakened body find strength to fight it? Would she lose him yet?

Susannah's mouth was dry with dread as the grim possibility looked her full in the face.

What would she do? If John left her, how would she manage here on this harsh prairie homestead? The thought of their five children, for whom she was responsible, haunted her. How could she care for them alone? Or keep them together? This last thought caused her a new fear. What if she was forced by necessity to place their children in other homes?

From here her thoughts took on a mind of their own. Unbidden, she recalled her own life as such a child. The bad memories, the beatings, the never quite fitting in, the verbal abuse, and then the other... Susannah shuddered.

Oh, she would do anything to protect her own children from that! But what if she had no control over what happened?

Her fears feasted on her anguished mind. Without thinking, she pulled back the covers on John, and mechanically began to freshen the plaster she had only administered shortly before. If slathering his skin with the goo would help the awful rattle deep within his chest, then she would do it—and do it often. The doctor had said she should keep on, hadn't he? Well then, she would.

John's eyes were closed. She couldn't tell if he was asleep or only trying to rest. Or if he wasn't really conscious. For sometimes he talked and his words made no sense.

These episodes were especially unnerving to her. Then she didn't know how to respond. To hear her usually calm, quiet-natured John rattling on in jumbled sentences frightened her each time he did so.

Automatically she felt his forehead. It felt warm. Too warm. She wondered how long the fever would last. No one could tell her.

No one could tell her anything. Susannah realized this truth with a new wave of vulnerable feelings. Only God knew if John would survive this sickness. Or if she would survive if he didn't.

On one hand she wished she could step outside and be suddenly far away from this awful strain. On the other, she knew there was nowhere else she would rather be than here, by John's side, taking care of him the best she could. Here where she would be the first to know when he took a turn for the better. Or for the worse.

chapter 34

Feeble Trust

The days passed in a blur for Susannah as John lay sick, his body fighting to conquer the fever that ran rampant through his cells. In a daze she cared for baby Joseph and supervised the others.

Emmanuel's sons took over the milking and the heaviest chores, for which Susannah was deeply grateful. Most of her waking hours she hovered close to her stricken husband. At times when John coughed that ragged, deep cough, she was close enough that the pain seemed to tear at her own chest. Sometimes she filled her own lungs deeply with air, wishing that John's shallow breaths could absorb some of the oxygen. She bathed his feverish face with cool cloths, but in only moments she would need to pile another woolen blanket onto his shivering body.

She was vaguely aware of prayers that passed from her thoughts to her Father in heaven. Her mind was too tense and weary to offer up structured prayer. At one point during which she believed John was nearing the end of his life, she wondered whether it was because she hadn't clarity of mind to pray as intensely as she ought to. Then she recalled dimly that somewhere in Scripture a verse stated that the Spirit knew what His children needed, and would make intercession for them with groanings which couldn't be uttered. This brought comfort to her weary heart. It freed her from the guilt of not being able to concentrate on praying. It meant she could continue to focus on caring for John—on doing everything she could think of that might aid him in fighting the battle he waged.

✳   ✳

Finally the fever relented. It left John alive, but so spent and weak that Susannah dared not hope he would ever be strong again. The cough continued. At the doctor's orders, John was to sip a glass of wine every day.

Susannah could not recall ever living through a winter as long as this one. Despite the circumstances, she did her best to keep her spirits strong. John's morale must be kept up, and the children must be kept quiet so he could rest. At the same time, she herself felt the need of a strong, comforting tonic of some kind.

Her thoughts traveled back to those long-ago times in Canada when Betsy's sweet voice rising in song would lift her spirit in a way nothing else could. Memories of those years seemed now almost to belong to another lifetime. Life had been hard then. It was still hard. With John, herself, and their children living on a prairie, there were challenges every day. Challenges in which one never knew for sure which would prevail: life or death, peace or turmoil.

The hymns she had learned from Betsy and from her own short time with the young folks now took on fresh, deep meaning for Susannah. She sensed that it soothed John if she sang softly. A few times he even attempted to join in, but each time a fresh spasm of coughing attacked his efforts.

John also liked the slow German hymns sung at church.

"It seems like a long time since we've been in church," he said wistfully to Susannah one day.

"Yes. It's been longer than usual, even for wintertime," she agreed. For services were sporadic anyway during winter weather.

Neither of them talked of the community problems. The close call with John's sickness nearly made that seem trivial.

From the bottom of her heart Susannah was grateful to their Lord for sparing John's life. Even as she was thankful, she couldn't help but wonder if he'd recover fully enough to do rigorous farmwork this coming spring and summer, if ever. She wondered how they would make a living for their growing family if he couldn't.

Still, he was by her side, and for that she worshiped the God who saved him. Surely, God would work out some way for them to make a living. He had worked in amazing ways before, even when there seemed no way out. She wanted to trust that He would do so again.

Shoving aside the worries of their situation, she softly began the words of the song "Glory Gates."

Looking up, her eyes met John's. He smiled. She knew this was one of his favorite hymns. For now she would sing. There was no use in worrying.

The melody and the words rose from her heart to her lips, and she brought all their needs to those "Glory Gates." To the one who could deal out whatever He saw as best.

That God did hear, and was preparing a way for them even now, was very true. Susannah would have been shocked had the plan been known to her.

But she did not know, and the future remained safely locked away from their eyes for another day. She did her best at trusting, even though she couldn't see a way yet.

chapter 35

Moving Plans

"Well, Susannah, what do you say? Shall we go, or shall we stay?" John posed the question to his wife when he arrived home from the trip he'd taken by train to visit Pennsylvania.

Susannah, very relieved to have her husband at home again, scarcely knew how to answer.

When several of the community men saw a lull in their summer's work, they made plans for the trip. John, who hadn't yet regained his former vigor since having been so sick the previous year, was invited to travel with them.

The men made no secret of the purpose of their trip. They wanted to see what Pennsylvania could offer. If things fell into place, they planned to take it as an indication of God's leading to move away from May City.

Now, here was John, safely at her side again, and asking her opinion. She truthfully didn't know what to say.

"What is it like?" she asked, putting off her answer to John's question.

"The land, you mean?"

"Yes," Susannah answered, though this was only the beginning of what she wanted to know.

"The land is interesting!" John replied with a chuckle. "There are hills, plenty of them. The Susquehanna River flows right through the community. So do lots of small creeks. There are trees aplenty. The fields are sort of, how would you say, tucked in among the hills, maybe? They say the land is poor, not fertile like we're used to here in Iowa." John paused.

Susannah waited, processing what he'd said.

In a moment or two John continued. "There are fruit trees, and they were starting to pick apples!" He couldn't hide the note of pleasure in his voice. "I ate quite a few," he said. The twinkle in his eyes told Susannah that he'd enjoyed them immensely.

"They don't have tornadoes there." He paused, then added softly, "And the church brethren seem to be at peace with each other."

Though he'd waited until last to share these two details, Susannah knew both were as important to her husband as to herself.

"Why don't we go, then?" she responded. For he had asked her what she thought.

John was quiet. Susannah knew he would make no snap decisions.

"I want to discuss it with my dad and brothers," was his response. "It's important to me to know what they think."

"Yes, do that," Susannah agreed. John's family had helped out greatly while John was so sick, and it would be unfair not to show them the courtesy of discussing such a serious plan.

Then, womanlike, her mind sped on to other details of practical life. "Where would we live? Could you find work? Would we buy a farm?" The questions tumbled over each other.

"That would all need to be worked out," John answered. He drew a deep breath. "A lot must still be worked out."

❋   ❋

In the coming weeks and months, prayers for wisdom and guidance flew heavenward. Advice was asked from family and brethren. Letters were written to Pennsylvania.

Details were hashed and possibilities rehashed until Susannah was weary of it. The children, not knowing what was to come, had a multitude of questions. Susannah couldn't answer them all, for she didn't know all the answers either.

Is it always this way when one makes a big change in life? Susannah asked herself one day as she prepared the familiar cornbread for their daily use. *Does one ever know for sure which step God wants one to take? Is it always so frightening to start over in life?* One could look to the past for examples and experiences, but one could never know what lies ahead.

When at last the decision was made to move to Pennsylvania, Susannah could scarcely believe it, nor grasp the magnitude of it. Israel and Emma Bauman would make the move at the same time. That was a comforting thought.

"It wouldn't surprise me if Emmanuel's moved too," John said one day. "But not just yet."

"What about your parents?" Susannah asked.

"Father is in favor of it. The thought of moving back to Pennsylvania where he originally came from appeals to him. I believe he still needs to convince Mother though," John said slowly.

Now that their plans were public, lots of people offered to help get the work done that goes with moving. John planned to do as the others had who previously moved away. He would make a public auction to sell their possessions and livestock. Then the family and a few necessary furniture items would travel to Pennsylvania by train. He wanted to get the plans in motion to make the move this coming winter.

Susannah's memories of her move to Iowa crowded in. Then it had only been herself and John, starting out with little to their name. Now there was lots to get rid of. Surely God had blessed them in spite of hard times.

John had been a hard worker, and it had paid off. It was hard for him to accept that he could no longer do the strenuous work that was once a joy to him.

Though Susannah had no personal family ties here in May City, she knew it would be harder for John to pull up the stakes. He would miss going to the lake to fish. It was special to him to come home after a day at the lake with a wagon load of fish. He would also miss going on a day trip by wagon to the Ocheyedan Mound. That landmark rose from the prairie like a strange hill. Some supposed it was a mound left by a glacier. It was a sacred place to the Indians who once roamed the prairie. They went to the mound to mourn their dead. When one was atop the vast mound, on the dished surface of it, one nearly felt like a part of the sky. Rolling prairie stretched out in all directions until it met the hazy sky on the horizon. Susannah never quite knew what John found so special about the mound. She had climbed to the summit with him one day, but the feeling of being so close to the sky made her feel uneasy. She'd been glad to descend, and walked thankfully back to the wagon. John had many boyhood memories of this prairie home before she'd ever gotten to know him.

But now they were moving to Pennsylvania! Why, that was nearly as far away as Iowa had been when she moved here from Canada. To her it would all be new territory again. She recalled a long-ago conversation with Betsy. One in which her girlish curiosity was stirred by talks of pioneers who'd moved north to Canada from Pennsylvania. She and Betsy had both agreed it unlikely that she would ever see that state.

With a wry smile, Susannah wondered what Betsy would say if she knew of their plans to move there soon.

Closing Out

PUBLIC SALE

As I am going east, I will offer at public sale on the N. E. quarter of section 4, Harrison township, 12 miles north of Hartley, 4 miles east and 5 1-2 south of Ocheyedan, 1 1-2 miles east and one north of May City, on

Wednesday, January 8th

Commencing at 10 o'clock, the following described property:

---

7   Head of Horses   7

Consisting of one black mare 9 years old, weight 1350; one gray gelding 4 years old, weight 1250; one bay gelding 9 years old, weight 1200; one bay gelding 8 years old, weight 1100; one sorrel mare, weight 1150; one bay colt coming two years old; one bay colt coming one year old.

13   Thoroughbred Short Horns   13

Headed by Sire 362446, out of Queen Anna 5634, trace to Imp Arabella by North Star (460.) Most of the young stock is of his get Consists of 5 cows giving milk now, 2 heifers coming 2 years old, 2 heifers coming one year old, one bull 9 months old, one bull 7 months old, one bull 3 months old. Pedigrees furnished with all the above mentioned cattle.

18   Grade Cattle   18

Consisting of 7 milk cows, 4 fresh now others fresh soon; 2 steers coming 2 years old, 3 steers coming one year old, 2 heifers coming two years old, 4 calves.

12   Chester White Shoats 4 Months Old   12

Machinery : Consisting of two lumber wagons, 1 truck wagon, 1 6-ft. Standard Deering binder, 1 corn binder, 1 8-ft. Osborne disc, almost new, 2 6-shovel corn plows, 1 John Deere surface cultivator, 1 bob sled, 1 16-shoe press drill, 1 John Deere hay loader, 1 McCormick mower 5 ft-cut, 1 Great Western manure spreader, 1 Hayes corn planter with 120 rods of wire, 1 16-ft drag, 1 18-ft. drag, 1 hay rack, one grindstone, 1 Cook Stove, 5 dozen chickens, etc.

40 bu. Seed Barley   Some Potatoes   300 bu. Good Corn in Crib

---

TERMS: Credit to Dec. 1, 1913, on approved note at 8 percent from date of sale

Free Lunch at Noon

JOHN BRUBAKER, Prop'r

P. A. Leese, Auctioneer   W. M. Roth, Clerk

chapter 36

Leaving Iowa

"Here are the sale flyers," John said to his wife upon returning home from town.

"Oh, let me see them." Susannah wiped her hands on her apron first, then picked up one of the papers John had laid on the table.

Her eyes flew across the bold black words. Seeing it in black and white on such official looking paper finally made it seem real.

John, thorough as always, had given directions to their farm. Then the date: Wednesday, January 8, followed by a precise listing of his horses, cattle, hogs, and machinery.

Susannah marveled again at the evidence of what had been accumulated in their eleven years here in Iowa. Yes, God had been good. They should be able to finish paying the doctor bills and have enough left after the sale to make the move without borrowing.

But there wouldn't be enough extra to buy a place right away in Pennsylvania. John had warned her of this. With his uncertain health, he was reluctant to go in debt to do so.

Hard times were surely not over for them, but if only they could live in a community with a strong, united leadership, both of them believed the Lord would take care of their material needs.

Her mind whirling with all these details, Susannah laid the sale flyer back on the pile.

The days leading up to January 8th were filled to the brim. John, with help from Emmanuel and his sons, worked to get the machinery oiled, cleaned, and in line.

For Susannah there was endless sorting and preparations for the day of the auction. It was customary for the owner to provide lunch for the buyers.

Usually it was simple: hot soup, a sandwich, coffee, and pie. Susannah asked a few neighborhood girls to serve the food. Mary and Magdalena would watch young Joseph.

She decided to send Amanda and Enoch to a neighbor for the day. With all the goings on, there would be no one to keep an eye on Enoch. The house would be hard to keep warm, with people in and out all day, and he would get cold.

"I want to stay home," wailed Amanda, upon hearing her mother's plan. "I'm big enough to help with something!"

"You need to go with Enoch and keep him occupied," Susannah replied firmly. "Maybe I can save you a bun with bologna on it for your supper."

At this Amanda brightened. Bread was a treat, and especially so if there was bologna on it!

"What if people eat all of it?" she couldn't help but ask.

"I'll save you some," Susannah promised.

With this Amanda had to be satisfied.

✻   ✻

January 8th arrived. Both John and Susannah were up long before dawn. Susannah's mind swam dizzily with all there was to do. There was no time to dawdle. The children were roused and dressed in all the layers they owned.

After Amanda and Enoch were escorted to the neighbors, Susannah put soup on the stove, and made plenty of sandwiches. She also made sure there was enough hot water for coffee.

Auctions were usually attended by men and boys. The women stayed home, keeping their own fires warm. A few came to help with the lunch, and for them Susannah was grateful.

The day wasn't as miserable as it could have been. At least the wind was gentle. The cold weather could be tolerated if the wind didn't drive it through every fiber of one's clothes.

The auction took place outdoors, with the animals being sold in the barn. At least during that time the crowd of buyers had shelter.

Susannah, busy in the kitchen, didn't know how things were going outside. Her duties in serving food left her no time to ask John if the sales were satisfactory. She would find out once it was all over.

She enjoyed the companionship of the other women in the kitchen. Soon enough she would be among strangers again, not knowing anyone.

In the next few days, Susannah realized their move would pull on her heartstrings more than she'd thought. One thing she would miss was their house, lovingly built for her by her new husband, John. Would they ever live in another one as special? Here in these very rooms the children had been born, and grew to take their first shaky steps. She enjoyed the view from her lean-to kitchen, from where she could see John when he was hard at work in the fields. Across the lane in the other direction, it wasn't far to John's parents' house. Wistfully she realized she had never known the blessings of a family until John willingly shared his. She'd certainly miss all of them.

The things she wouldn't miss were easier to reflect on. One was those dreadful tornadoes, with their sudden fury. There were many other things too. The ever-present wind which blasted for no reason at all. The lack of trees and fruit. The harsh winters. The long distance to town. The scarcity of doctors. And perhaps more than anything else, the lack of unity in the church. What would it be like to live in a settlement with a brotherhood of harmony?

John had talked of this late into the night recently. She had no doubts as to how important this was to him. But, as he'd said, each group is bound to have their own struggles. Because wherever there is a good thing, like peace, Satan will try to destroy it. So while they certainly hoped things would be better in Pennsylvania, they were not so naive as to think everything would be a bed of roses.

Finally the day arrived. Excitement fevered the girls. They couldn't imagine boarding a train. They had no qualms about leaving their only home behind. For them it was an adventure such as they had only dreamed of until now.

Finally each one was settled in the wagon bed. John handed Joseph to her. Then he climbed to the seat, wrapped in so many layers that his movements were slow and stiff.

The team was eager to be on the way. White steam rolled from their nostrils into the cold pre-dawn January air. A neighbor man would drive the team and wagon back from Ocheyedan once the family boarded the train.

Shifting Joseph's body, Susannah turned for one last look at her home. The wagon rolled out of the yard, and she could barely make out the dark shape of the house. No warm white smoke plume curled from the chimney, for they'd sold the stove. No pulse of lantern light glowed from the windows. All was silent, cold, and dark.

She was glad the children couldn't see the tears that spilled from her eyes. The squeal of wheels on packed snow masked the children's chatter. Soon darkness hid their buildings. Or were they already behind a knoll? Susannah turned her face forward. She willed her mind to look forward as well.

chapter 37

On the Train

The wait was over. In front of them rumbled the massive train. The men had already taken care of the load of furnishings to be put on the freight car. Susannah had forgotten how the ground itself trembled underneath the weight and power of the mighty train, with its belching engines.

It was too much for three-year-old Enoch. Terrified by the monster in front of him, he refused to board the steps leading to the passenger car.

"Here, let William go first," spoke up Israel Bauman. "Maybe then Enoch will follow."

This did the trick. Seeing the other lad bravely step up into the coach, Enoch was game to follow suit.

After a flurry of directions to the girls, they were all on board. By the time Susannah had found seats for all of her family, the train had begun to move.

Emma was also busy seating her brood. Israel and John busied themselves stowing up boxes of food and personal luggage.

Susannah was again grateful that they weren't the only family moving away. Already she felt that lonely, unattached feeling of being between homes. It would be good to have another family arriving in Snyder County, Pennsylvania, with them.

The conductor checked their tickets. He paused a moment to count the children, then spoke a few pleasant words to them before he continued up the narrow center aisle of the car.

Susannah overheard the girls' awestruck whispers as they examined their surroundings. She couldn't help but smile at their excited words.

"Just look at these fine seats!" Mary exclaimed. "Such a lovely red!"

"Oh, yes!" Magdalena breathed. "And such soft fabric!" She ran her hands reverently along the velvety back of their seat. "My! I'm going to like traveling by train!"

Susannah knew they'd seldom, if ever, seen such luxurious fabric. She only hoped that they would still like the seats as well by the time the long trip turned into boredom.

Settling into her own seat, Susannah's eyes took in the prairie rolling past the train window on her left. Would she ever return to this part of Iowa? She doubted it. As her gaze took in the expanse of treeless land, she rejoiced that Pennsylvania would have trees. According to John, plenty of them! Maybe they could even plant fruit trees and grow their own fruit! Her thoughts turned to wistful dreams as her tired body rested from the furious pace of preparations the last few days.

Swaying, creaking, and clacking its way eastward, the train lulled her passengers to sleep as it sped along the iron rails.

By dawn the next day they neared Chicago. The children had never seen a city before.

"What are those bright lights along the streets?" Mary asked.

"They're electric lamps," replied John.

"How do they work? Does someone light them like our lanterns?"

Susannah listened half-heartedly as John attempted to explain to their prairie-born children how modern electricity worked. He pointed out the high wires that were fastened to poles along the streets. But the children couldn't grasp the idea that current could travel into the lamps from that.

Recalling the vast depot in Chicago, Susannah dreaded their stop there. They would need to change to another train for the rest of the trip. How could she keep track of all the children while John took care of their baggage? She decided on firm direction before they unloaded. "Now, listen. You must stay close to me when we get into the station! Father will make sure the freight gets switched to the right train. If any of you wander away and lose yourself, we'll travel on to Pennsylvania without you. Girls, you must watch Enoch! Don't lose sight of him!"

They nodded, wide-eyed. Susannah hoped the warning had registered.

Apparently it had. Upon disembarking, John led them to the station and directed them into a corner. Mary and Magdalena each kept a hand linked into Enoch's. With Amanda clutching her skirt, Susannah held Joseph firmly in her own arms.

"Wait right here," John advised. "I'll get you something to eat. Then I'll see about our things."

Before long he returned. He handed a brown paper bag to Susannah. Then he set down a tray with steaming cups of coffee.

With anticipation she looked into the bag. Donuts! With excited squeals the children accepted them. This was a rare treat for them.

"Shall we save ours?" Magdalena asked of her older sister, Mary.

"Maybe," Mary replied, pondering the delicacy a moment. "But I'm very hungry!" This was the deciding factor.

Susannah was grateful for the distraction of the food while they waited for John to return. It seemed to take him a long time and she began to wonder if he had gotten lost. The donuts and coffee were long gone. The children watched the crowd of people swirling around them in amazement. They had never seen so many people at once.

All these people thronging through the station made Susannah nervous. Where were they all going? Where had they all come from? And how confident they all appeared! The longer they waited for John, the more ill at ease she felt. She watched the hands on the large clock on the wall high above their heads. What was she going to do if John didn't come soon? It was nearly time to board the eastbound train.

"Where is Father?" This question from Amanda voiced Susannah's own tense thoughts.

"Surely he'll come soon." She tried to sound hopeful in spite of her fear.

A tall man approached from out of the crowd. Susannah saw him, but didn't look closely. A glance told her it wasn't John, for John wore a full beard.

The man walked confidently up to them.

Susannah, wondering at his brashness, lifted her eyes for a closer look at him.

Those eyes! The familiar twinkle! But such hollow cheeks. Her thoughts raced in circles through her confused mind. Why was the face before her so oddly familiar?

"Father?" Mary's disbelieving word seemed to come from a long way off.

"John!" Susannah gasped.

He grinned mischievously.

"Are you ready to go, girls? Shall we get in line, Enoch? What say, Susannah?" John addressed them all. Seeing they had nothing to say seemed to amuse him.

"Father doesn't have his beard anymore." This fact was calmly stated by Amanda.

Ignoring their staring eyes, John herded them out to the railyard. It was time to board the train to Pennsylvania. Questions could be answered once they settled in for the next long leg of the trip.

Once more Susannah was grateful for John's keen sense of direction. She would have gotten lost in the maze of people, trains, and noise.

Finally, they were on board and clickety-clacking eastward again. Settling into their seat, Susannah at last had an opportunity to really look at her husband.

That he had shaved off his beard while they waited was obvious. His face now looked so lean. Almost thin. It would take some getting used to. John turned to meet her gaze.

His eyes are still the same, though, Susannah thought gratefully. John's kind expression had always made him attractive to her.

"What do you think?" John asked finally.

"It will be different," was all Susannah could think to say.

"Yes, it will. But we want to be respectful and cooperative," was John's reply.

Susannah nodded. John's words and example were a blessing to her. The beard, or lack of one, had been a major point of contention in May City. John, having come from Canada where beards were normal, had continued to wear his. Others in the community had convictions against facial hair. Bishop Bauman took no stand for either side, and there was no unity in this, or in other matters. Now they had pulled up stakes and were moving to Snyder County, Pennsylvania, where all the men were clean-shaven. For various reasons that decision had been reached and upheld.

John concluded that community peace was more important than having a beard. Thus he had taken time to shave and be as ready as he could, both outwardly and inwardly, before they reached their destination.

"We want to live in a setting of unity and love among our fellowmen, don't we?" he asked his wife.

"Yes," Susannah agreed heartily.

"So we want to be careful lest our own opinions or ideas are a stumbling block to others. Especially since we are newcomers into an established area." John spoke slowly. "We've seen how it goes in a settlement where two sides don't agree and neither gives in."

As she mulled over his words, Susannah saw the wisdom of them. If they truly desired a life in a stable environment, then everyone had a part to do. That meant herself and John, as well as anyone else.

Part III

chapter 38

Snyder County, Pennsylvania

The children, having slept more on the train than Susannah was able to, were filled with anticipation. They were nearly at their new home!

They were to have temporary quarters with the Absalom Tharp family. That this was a former May City family was small comfort to Susannah. Having left his first wife behind in the cemetery on the Iowa prairie, Abs had by now remarried. His second wife, Mary, was a stranger to Susannah.

Though grateful for the arrangement of immediate shelter after the long journey, she dreaded the daily sharing of a stranger's home. Rather than dwell on the subject, Susannah took in the scenery as the wagon rolled along. They had gotten off the train at Sunbury and were now on the last leg by wagon. The air was fresh and bracing after so many days of stale train air. Though cold, it felt like a milder cold than that of Iowa.

And the trees! Susannah couldn't drink in enough of them with her tired eyes. Trees, hills, and rushing, tumbling creeks at nearly the base of every hill. Snow covered the creek banks, making the water look dark and icy. Fields and pastures looked like nearly an afterthought.

Rows of corn stubble marched up the sides of a hill, and then down the slope toward the creek. It was different, for sure. But in her heart Susannah rejoiced. Here one might surely blend in!

For a time, the wagon passed alongside the Susquehanna. John had told her of this large river. Large mountains loomed on the far side of it. Their wintry tree-clad sides looked gray and dismal. Susannah wondered how it would look to see them wearing green in the summer. Large rocks jutted out of the riverbed at intervals, causing the water to swirl around them in their journey to larger waters. What obstacles might yet cause ripples like that in their future, Susannah wondered?

At last they arrived at the Tharp home. Susannah was glad to be there. The journey had been wearying. But now they were to be settled in at the mercy of someone else's hospitality.

A cheerful, bustling Mary ushered them in. "My," she chatted. "Aren't you cold? Do come in and we'll get you warmed up. You must be nearly frozen! Such a long trip!"

"We're used to the cold," John informed her calmly.

After greetings were over and the children settled close to the big stove, Mary showed Susannah the arrangements. They were to have the wash house for their living quarters. Bedrooms were prepared for them in the attic above the main floor.

"You may stay with us as long as you need to, John," Absalom offered. "It might be hard to find work or a suitable home until spring. Until then, you may use what we have, though it's not much."

"We appreciate this," John responded sincerely.

It felt good to sleep in a real bed again, with no lurching, creaking train to contend with. The attic rafters showed, but that didn't deter the children, who fell asleep only moments after hitting the bed.

✳   ✳

It didn't take long to get settled into their temporary quarters, and the children wasted no time in exploring the outdoor surroundings.

"Stay back from the riverbanks," Susannah warned. "The water is deep. We don't want any of you to drown!"

"I can't see how they can stay outside so long," Mary Tharp marveled.

"It's so cold!"

"But Iowa is much colder," insisted Amanda. "This seems warm! Besides, we're wearing lots of clothes!"

Not long after their arrival in Snyder County they received a visitor—an unwelcome one.

Young Mary was the first to notice it. "My eyes are so tired," she said one day.

Susannah thought probably her daughter hadn't gotten enough rest during the strenuous move. Then Amanda commented that her throat felt swollen. This was cause for alarm. Susannah felt both girls' foreheads. They felt hot. She began to administer tonics and plasters for their throat and chest, but in spite of everything she did, their fever mounted. Coughing and sneezing, both girls were sent up the narrow attic stairway to their beds.

"My, I hope this doesn't last long," Susannah thought. "It's a long trip up those stairs to take care of them."

Two days later Mary developed small, itchy red spots on her skin.

"Measles," said Mary Tharp grimly.

Susannah gasped. Why hadn't she thought of that? Of course! Now it all made sense. In this case she would indeed get well acquainted with that stairway. The two sick girls must be kept away from the others, lest they pass on the germ.

Later she couldn't say how they made it through the winter. One after the other the children all got the measles.

Fever wracked their bodies. Any bit of light coming in through the window hurt their eyes. Swollen glands nearly choked them. Appetites disappeared. As soon as the rash subsided, then the itchy peeling of the skin began.

Thankfully young Joseph had a mild case. Susannah didn't know how she would have coped had he been as feverish as the older ones.

Mary Tharp, instead of avoiding them as she might rightfully have done, sent many a bowl of soup over to Susannah's wash house domain. This was a blessing, as there was scarcely any time or energy on Susannah's part to prepare food.

"'I'll make sure to boil the bowls before I return them," Susannah said. "We don't want you to get the measles too."

"Oh, we've already had them," Mary said. "That's the only good thing about measles!"

Finally the children recovered, but it seemed a slow process to their anxious mother. Not until spring had begun to tint the hills in pale green was everyone feeling well again.

chapter 39

Relocating

The hills gradually changed into a dusty shade of green, then as more buds unfurled in the warm sunshine they became vibrant with new life. Showers of rain that gently fell upon the hillsides softened the earth and soon myriads of blossoms appeared in the balmy air.

When John came home one evening after work he had news. "There's a place available close to the church house, Susannah," he said. "Shall we go ahead and see if it works out to move up there?"

"Oh, that would be nice," Susannah said in reply.

Supper was a meager meal. The money John earned as a day laborer had to be stretched to cover many needs. It would be nice to live where they could grow their own garden, and also have some livestock and chickens to supply their own meat, milk, and eggs.

"You say close to the church?" she asked after some thought.

"Yes. The place just below the church. I think you might like it," John said. "If I remember right, there's a creek running close to the buildings."

"Could we be there in time to put in a garden and crops?"

"We'll see. I sure hope so," John agreed.

John did see about the matter as soon as he could. It seemed as though it was meant to be. Plans were made to move in time to get a good start with seedtime.

Susannah was grateful. Though it had been generous of the Tharps to offer them a place to live, it wasn't like having a home of their own.

So it was with high hopes that they made the move to their new home. The children too were excited. As they unloaded and settled into the house, it was exciting to arrange their own table and chairs. Beds were made in rooms that they hoped could remain theirs for a long time to come.

It had been an exhausting time for Susannah. With great weariness she settled down to sleep under their own roof for the first time since leaving Iowa.

Her gratitude, however, was just as great as her weariness. This was the new beginning she and John had long hoped and prayed for. Like the fresh new growth of spring, they hoped for a new opportunity to raise their children to the glory of the Lord.

The Susquehanna River, running boisterously not far from the house, held a deep fascination for the children. It was much too close for Susannah's comfort. It took daily vigilance to make sure the children respected the mighty waterway.

The move to their new home was just in time. On the second of May a new baby daughter joined the family. They named her Nancy, after John's mother, Nancy Anna.

With great joy everyone welcomed the newcomer. Susannah had feared for the unborn baby when the rest of the family suffered from the measles this past winter, but here she was, healthy and apparently unscathed. It was almost too much to grasp. God had indeed been merciful to them.

The new baby served to blend the family into the community. It was customary for families to go visit at homes with a new arrival. This provided an excellent way for John and Susannah to get to know their neighbors and fellow church members.

It also gave Susannah the opportunity to ask advice from other women. At first baby Nancy appeared fine and healthy, but as time went on, she began to cry inconsolably. Susannah herself couldn't comfort her, and eating did nothing to alleviate the infant's misery. Maybe the women who had more experience could offer guidance. It was all to no avail.

At last the doctor decided the baby had rickets. This was why she remained frail and so unhappy. Upon doctor's orders, they began to get milk from one of the neighbors to feed the tiny girl. Slowly a difference could be seen. Though she remained small, Nancy at least was no longer so pathetically thin.

John's parents were by now also living in Snyder County. Susannah knew it was a relief to John. To her, it was also special. Now they too had family in the community.

Grandfather Jacob's comment upon seeing the sickly little Nancy warmed Susannah's heart. "Ach," he said, "she'll be all right. Wait till she puts some 'speck' on her ribs."

His words proved true. Nancy's little body began to absorb the nutrients from the milk, and before long one couldn't tell she'd had such a rough beginning.

John struggled to earn a living. Being sick so long in Iowa had taken a toll on his health. By the time the rent was paid for, there was often little left of his wages. Then, too, the hilly terrain of Snyder County didn't yield crops or vegetables like the fertile, black Iowa soil. Susannah could tell he longed to enrich the soil and build up the ground in hopes of a higher yield, but he was reluctant to do so on property not his own.

When John learned that the next farm just down the valley was for sale, he was immediately interested. With his father's encouragement, plans were made to buy it. At least the move wasn't far and the children could continue to attend the same school.

Susannah was still trying to get used to yet another house when baby Leah came in October of 1913. She was a joy, and the older sisters vied for the chance to hold her at any opportunity.

The days were hardly long enough to get the work done. With Mary, Magdalena, and Amanda attending school, Susannah often got little else done besides caring for the baby and eighteen-month-old Nancy.

This left Joseph time to devise mischief. Susannah's only helper was Enoch, who could help with small chores, if he so chose.

John was so busy it seemed she seldom saw him. At last he had a place upon which to plant the fruit trees he'd so long dreamed of. Having chosen the sloping hillside beyond the barn, John planted cherry trees, plum trees, and rows of apple trees. Carefully he chose the varieties. Tart Jonathans for pies, King David for snitz and drying, and large Pound apples just for the joy of eating them.

Still not done, he planted apricot and more plum trees behind the house. Susannah enjoyed his pleasure in this. She knew that if the trees didn't bear fruit, it wouldn't be because John hadn't taken enough pains to tend them.

When this was done, he began the work of improving his land. Scrimping in some other areas, he ordered loads of lime to be put on the fields and pastures. Having had the pile dumped close to the barn, he now spent hours shoveling it onto the wagon and then flinging it one shovelful at a time across the depleted soil of his new farm.

No, Susannah mused, *if we can't make a go of it here, it won't be because John hasn't done his best.*

chapter 40

Dark Memories

The stalwart hills of Snyder County offered a sense of protection that Susannah cherished. A stability seemed to ooze from the unmovable hills. They blocked out disturbing winds such as those she had so disliked in Iowa.

Nothing, however, kept the winds of change from filtering into their lives. Talk that drifted into the community from the outside world was disturbing. European countries were having problems: serious ones. Many had already declared war on each other. Woodrow Wilson, the new president of the United States, didn't yet have a confident following. People were divided in their opinions of what he should do. Some fervently hoped he wouldn't get the United States involved in the battle overseas, while others believed he should.

The Mennonite community waited uneasily for the outcome. Whatever would come, they would try to uphold the teachings of Jesus. Past experiences with wartimes hadn't left good memories. If it became reality, there were sure to be hard times ahead.

In the course of time President Wilson did get the United States involved. By now so many countries were entangled in the bloody conflict that people referred to it as the Great War or World War.

Susannah shuddered at hearing stories that came from large newspapers. What horrors of fighting starvation, and bloodshed! Why must human beings act like this? Why did the struggle for power always victimize the innocent?

In July of 1915, death cast its dark shadow upon their lives when John's father, Jacob S. Brubaker, entered that rest into which the living cannot enter. His sixty-nine years of life had ended here, close to where he'd been born. His life's journey had taken a long, toilsome circle. Up to Canada with the pioneering group who attempted to carve a beginning in that wilderness, then west to Iowa to help start another community in that harsh climate. Finally the move back to Snyder County.

He was buried on the slope of a hillside close to the meetinghouse. The quiet murmur of the creek nearby seemed a fitting song for the final resting place of his earthly body. Susannah knew Jacob would be sorely missed. He had offered much sound advice and encouragement to herself and John over the years. That, and also financial aid.

Seeing how John struggled to regain a profitable farming operation here, Jacob had bought them a silo. It made an unbelievable difference. With that additional feed to sustain them during winter months, the milk production of their cows increased. So had the cash flow of their income. How could they ever be grateful enough for the kindness of this man who was now laid to rest?

It was still a struggle to make ends meet, however. As much as she disliked it, they decided to let the girls work away from home to bring in additional income. There always seemed to be neighboring families in need of a young maid to assist with manual labor.

Susannah doubted that John would ever realize how much she dreaded seeing them leave. Once they were away from home, she could no longer protect them. Memories of herself being subject to abuse of every kind haunted her. Why had her parents not tried harder to keep the family together? But now as a parent herself, she realized the struggle to keep food on the table.

The best she could do was to insist that her daughters come home every Saturday and Sunday. At least that way they could still be at home with their own family for part of the time. But the money they brought home definitely helped. Even the 50¢ a week earned by young Amanda came in handy.

News came from Canada one day. It informed Susannah that her father, John Heckendorn, had passed away in early December of 1916. This caused a wave of unbridled emotion for Susannah. John Heckendorn had never been a real father to her. She'd known all her life that she was one of his children, but that was all. And that fact had never brought comfort or stability. It was more often a taunt and a source of misery.

Family ties had been severed further by her own marriage to John Brubaker and their move to Iowa. Letters from Canada were scarce, and there had been no opportunity to return for a visit.

In 1917 she received another letter from Ontario. This news further saddened Susannah. This time it held news that her younger sister, Lydiann, had died of cancer. This fact was hard to grasp. Lydiann. Her sister. They hadn't grown up together, so there was no bond such as sisters often shared.

Dark questions swirled through Susannah's mind. Had life been kind to Lydiann? What of all the others? What of Israel, the youngest? Where was he by now? Was he even still alive? Did any of them remember her? Or did they think of her as they might recall a distant relative, instead of as a sister?

Betsy. The thought of the girl she had grown up with reminded Susannah that she had known the comradeship of a sister. There was no blood connection, but a linking of hearts. Betsy was the one person who actually knew what she'd endured, and she had done all she could to alleviate the suffering. How Susannah wished she could see her again! It was a futile wish, she knew, for too many miles and too little cash separated them.

If it hadn't been for Betsy, where might she be now? Susannah pondered again the many ways Betsy had shown her the love of Christ. Would she have given her heart to the Lord had it not been for Betsy? Bald truth stared at Susannah now. How easy it was for a person to be a seemingly upright and good church member and still harbor sin and evil in the heart! Even if she had ever gotten up the nerve to speak out against the awful things she had endured, hardly anyone would have believed her. Mr. and Mrs. Martin were too affluent in the neighborhood. On the surface, they were every way compliant with the church standards. Yes, had she spoken up about what really went on in that household, the daughter of poor John Heckendorn would have faced much more scorn and mockery.

Susannah swallowed the sick feelings these thoughts always created. Sick and dirty and helpless. Unworthy and used.

In spite of it all, Susannah knew there would be a righteous judgment. And until then she must bear the awful things that life had piled upon her plate. She must forgive. It was hard. The hardest part was that it must be done over and over. It was not a once done, victorious act. Even Jesus groaned upon the cross, "Father, forgive them, for they know not what they do."

She must focus on the ways in which God had blessed her life. Yes, blessed and protected and provided for her.

Thoughts of these blessings were like a balmy breeze to Susannah's troubled heart. Gloomy memories retreated to their shadowy closets again. She longed to be clean and pure and worthy. How she coveted the blood of Jesus! How she longed to be forgiving, and trust in her heavenly Father's truth and grace. And how she longed for her heart and life to be in harmony with the Word of God and His love.

She knew herself to be very human. Though others didn't know about the darkness in her heart and mind, she did. And God. Maybe no one really knew that the strain of keeping those memories hidden from human eyes was the very thing that caused her to be sharp with others. With John, even. With the children. And with herself.

The injustices were a secret between the Lord and herself. So it was to Him that she directed her plea for more love and patience with those in her life. To enable her to be more like Himself.

chapter 41

Baby Jacob

In the fall of 1918 the war ended. People sighed with relief and hoped for better days ahead. Lives had been lost and countries destroyed. Now would come the huge work of rebuilding and trying to go on in the aftermath of the horror. For many families things would never be the same, as loved ones would never return home.

In spite of new beginnings, there would remain many memories of those losses. But human nature is created by God to hope for better things, so people focused on the future, and life continued.

The year 1919 began with high hopes. It was also so for John and Susannah. In June a new baby came once more into their lives. With joy they named him Jacob.

But even before the doctor left, a shadow of fear for the child descended upon them. Something was wrong. There was an opening on the lower spine that shouldn't be there.

The doctor couldn't offer any hope of repairing the blemish.

"Take care of him, and keep it as clean as you can," were his words of advice. "If it gets infection in there..." His words trailed off.

Both John and Susannah sensed that what he'd left unsaid was crucial.

There is only one beautiful baby in all the world, and that's the one every mother has. Susannah couldn't get over tiny Jacob's perfect features. How soft his dark hair was!

The oldest girls wanted to hold him as much as they could. Leah, the youngest, at nearly six years old, would stroke his cheeks softly as she whispered to him.

Amanda, ever caring, and having a fascination for curing and healing, was sure that there must be something to be done for baby Jacob. Every liniment and salve they had was brought out and tenderly administered in hopes of helping him.

Jacob became feverish and cried pitifully. Soon an ominous dark red color circled the opening of his wound.

John begged the doctor to visit again.

With a grim expression on his face he examined the baby.

Susannah fought hard against her inner forebodings. Now that the doctor was here, surely he could give something to help. At least some straw of hope! Surely this beautiful baby hadn't been born only to suffer and die.

"We just don't have any medicine to cure infection." The doctor's words were gentle with sympathy. "I'd give anything if we had something to fight infection."

Susannah's prayers for the baby changed as his condition worsened. At first she'd wanted nothing more than to keep this child and love him with all the care she could give. She pleaded with God, who she knew had the ability to heal any sickness on earth. Her mother heart could hardly summon, "Thy will be done," at the end of her prayers.

As Jacob's condition worsened and his tiny body was wracked in merciless seizures, Susannah pleaded only for his spirit to be released from its sick little earthly form.

On June 19, eleven days after his birth, little Jacob died.

John's eyes spoke of his own deep grief as they made the final plans for their infant son. They would have only a simple burial service at the cemetery.

When they viewed his form one last time, Susannah's eyes hungrily drank in every detail of Jacob's angelic face. It felt as though the biggest part of her own heart would be buried with this baby, in his tiny coffin.

Other parents had faced trials like this, perhaps more than once. Susannah now realized that nothing had prepared her for this. How did others cope with this brutal reality?

Even as she longed to fill her arms with that tiny body in the days that followed, she reminded herself that Jacob was in a land of pure delight. There was no sickness, no pain, and no tears in heaven. These thoughts brought comfort, even though they did nothing to fill the void left in their home. He had only been with them such a short time, yet how empty it now seemed!

It was June, and summer with all its pulsing new life seemed a mockery to her. How could the season be so fresh and alive and vibrant when her baby was dead? John had to busy himself with field work, for a farm will not permit its owner the luxury of idle grief. It seemed he found solace in the demands of daily chores.

Susannah tried to concentrate on her garden and on caring for her other children. After all, they still needed her. Baby Jacob did not.

Sundays were hard, for these were a day of rest. Going to church meant passing the cemetery where they now had personal ties. It was a small comfort, however, to know that their baby's body lay close to his grandfather's grave. Somehow it seemed less lonely to think that they could rest together in the shade of the pines, with the soothing murmur of the creek nearby.

Susannah could almost picture the two up in heaven, exploring delights together. Would her baby still be a baby there? Would John's father still be an old man? Questions about heaven swirled through her mind. How she longed for a glimpse of her baby again!

Conversations among the women of the community nearly irked Susannah. They spoke of their summer work and the yield of their gardens and crops. She felt like reprimanding them for their mundane chatter. *Don't you know that life is vain? Don't you know that my child is dead? That nothing matters anymore? How can you go on as if nothing changed?* Her heart cries were silent, though at times she struggled mightily to keep it so.

They simply didn't understand. *Just as I didn't at one time,* she reminded herself.

John did though. Susannah knew his heart was pained at the loss, even though he bore it with stalwart outward strength. It was incredible how the death of their child drew their hearts together. John seemed to somehow always sense when she was struggling extra hard to accept her empty arms. The small kindnesses he showed her then warmed her heart to the core. On better days, she sometimes noticed when he was more quiet than usual and his eyes were dark with pain. Then it was her turn to reciprocate. After all, no other human being knew just what they had gone through. It was their grief, together. Susannah thanked the Lord for giving her a kind and loving husband. How would she cope with this trial if it weren't for John?

chapter 42

A Miracle for Joseph

When school started that fall, Susannah felt the loss keenly again. Even Leah now joined the others on their daily trek across the meadow, over the creek, and up the hill to Verdilla School. This left Susannah at home with no little ones to care for. Time stretched out in seemingly endless hours with unaccustomed quietness.

The school rules were that children must speak English in the classroom. The children, once they became fluent in English, began to speak it at home as well. John protested at this. "You must speak it there, to obey the teacher," he told them. "But here at home you will speak Dutch." He recalled too many instances where the Pennsylvania Dutch language had lost out for just such reasons. It pleased Susannah that John upheld the dialect of their fathers. She too had noticed that often once the language changed, so did other things that were even more precious.

In the evenings, John and Susannah enjoyed the happy chatter of the children and the interesting tidbits they brought home from school.

The schoolhouse and school yard were right next to Mr. Sechrist's store. The local people referred to him as "Siggy." It wasn't unusual for the children to bring home stories about the storekeeper.

Because the store business was sometimes slow, Siggy supplemented his income by giving haircuts to neighborhood men.

"Guess what?" Amanda proclaimed one evening at the supper table.

"Now what?" asked her father.

"There was a man at Siggy's store today wanting a haircut. But he was too tight to pay Siggy the 10-cent price. He complained about it so much that Siggy said, 'Okay. I'll give you one for 5 cents, then.'

"So the man got on the barber chair and Siggy clipped away. Soon he said, 'Okay, sir. There you go. That'll be 5 cents.' The man reached up to feel the job. 'But you only cut half my hair!' he protested.

"Siggy said, 'I know. I'll cut the other half for 5 cents too.'"

The family enjoyed a chuckle. No doubt the customer decided not to complain about the fee the next time he wanted a haircut on Siggy's chair.

Young Joseph didn't join in the chatter of the other scholars. Somehow he had never learned to talk correctly. His words came out in a jumble that almost no one understood. Even the family seldom understood his garbled sounds. In school he fell behind in studies because of his inability to communicate. The teacher gave up on him, and chose to focus on the many other students in the crowded classroom.

It pained Susannah. She was sure Joseph was a bright boy. But since he couldn't make others understand what he wished to say, they simply assumed he wasn't very smart. She wished fervently there was something she could do to help him.

Joseph, meanwhile, had nearly given up talking. It was too embarrassing when he couldn't get his point across. Rather than face frustrated looks of listeners, he simply remained silent.

Enoch, on the other hand, excelled in learning. This made Joseph appear especially simple.

Though John was a good father, Susannah sensed that even he considered Joseph as simple. *I wish John could see what he's doing,* she thought. *He takes such delight in showing Enoch how to do things. I wish he'd spend more time with Joseph too. It hurts Joe. I know it does. But what can I do about it?*

Susannah sometimes feared that being the apple of John's eye would ruin Enoch. What was a mother to do? Being a parent certainly wasn't easy.

One day the children came home from school all excited.

"Mother!" Amanda exclaimed. "Do you know what? A nurse came to school today and examined all the pupils. When she got to Joe and was looking into his mouth, she said, 'Oh, my! I've never seen anything like this.'" Amanda was breathless from running home so fast with her news.

"Yes. Then all the children crowded around him. They wanted to see what the nurse meant." Nancy joined in with more details.

"Well, what was it?" asked Susannah.

"She says he has an opening in the top of his mouth. If it were fixed, maybe he *could* talk!" Amanda's eyes were bright with hope. "She said you should take him to the doctor for surgery!"

"Well!" Susannah sat down abruptly. This was all a new idea. Maybe Joe's problem could be fixed! But surgery!

Joe himself was only now coming home. He had lagged behind the others as usual. His face looked stormy. No doubt the fuss at school had made him feel even more like a dunce.

"We'll talk to Father about it," Susannah said. The children sensed that the subject was closed for now.

Hope sprang up in Susannah's breast. If Joe could learn to talk clearly, others might accept him as normal. Then he wouldn't feel so pushed back. First John would have to be convinced of it, though.

As Susannah feared, he was reluctant, but he listened to the story of the school nurse's opinion. And it wasn't that Amanda didn't relate it convincingly.

Susannah's heart warmed while Amanda, ever the one in the family to be concerned about others, nearly begged John to take Joe to the doctor. *Maybe she can convince him better than I can,* thought Susannah.

Joseph was summoned. The family took turns peering into the top of his mouth. Yes, there was an opening there. But could it really be the root of his problem?

Later, in private, John voiced his doubts to his wife. "I just don't know, Susannah. Surgery would cost a lot. And what if it doesn't help his other problems?"

"What other problems?" It came out rather sharply.

"Well," John hesitated. "It seems he's not like the others." There. It was out.

"He's not like the others because he can't talk!" Susannah replied with more warmth than she had intended to. "If he was able to speak, he'd be just fine. He's not dim-witted, John! You shouldn't treat him as though he was."

"What do you mean?" John asked defensively.

"He gets pushed back, and you treat Enoch like a king—just because he learns fast. It's not fair!" Susannah was desperate for John to understand. Unfairness had left ugly scars in her own life, and she felt strongly that she must stand up for her son so he wouldn't suffer any more shame and ridicule. If there was something to be done for Joe, then she wholeheartedly wanted to have it done.

John listened patiently. This was what Susannah so appreciated about him. Once her thoughts were poured out, she sat waiting for his next words.

"Maybe we should," he said finally.

It took a while to make the arrangements. The doctor was very hopeful that he could help Joe by doing the surgery.

At last the day came. Susannah knew Joe was dreading it, even if he didn't express his fears. She felt sorry for him. Yet the hope for his improvement in the future tempered her sympathy.

When the surgery was over, Amanda took over the caregiving duties of her younger brother. She saw to it vigilantly that he regularly washed his mouth with a salt water solution.

Mary and Magdalena teased her for it. They called her "Nurse Amanda." And it was true. The girl had caregiving talents that would no doubt benefit her wherever life led her.

Joseph, however, didn't speak immediately. This worried Susannah. What if John was right? What if they had put him through all this and he still remained silent?

Susannah knew it takes time to heal wounds, but she was impatient. Oh, how she longed for their son to fit in! If the surgery was no success, then there was nothing more she could do for him. She took her concerns once more to the Lord. Where else could she go with her burdens? He knew and understood their daily concerns, and if He wanted to He could cause Joseph to speak.

Ever so slowly he began. At first the sounds he made were much like his previous ones. His tongue had to practice making the sounds of words now that his cleft palate was healed. It was a joy to see him gain confidence in speech. Now when he made a mistake, he would try again until those around him understood his sentences.

One day, weeks later, the scholars again came home with a story of Siggy, the storekeeper. This time it was Joe who told it.

"There was a customer at Siggy's store today," he said clearly. "He didn't want to bother tying his horse at the rail because he only wanted one thing at the store. Siggy was out on the store porch on his rocker. The man asked Siggy to watch his horse until he came back out. Siggy said he would. It didn't take the customer long to find what he wanted. When he came back out, Siggy was still rocking away, but the horse and wagon weren't there anymore.

"'You said you'd watch my horse for me!' the customer said angrily.

"'I *am* watching him,' Siggy said dryly. 'See, there he goes.' He pointed to a speck on the road that was rapidly getting smaller as the horse traveled toward home."

The family chuckled heartily. It was just like Siggy to do such a thing.

Susannah's look met John's eyes and was rewarded with a bright twinkle in their depths. His expression mirrored the thanksgiving in her own heart.

Not only had they enjoyed the tale, but it was extra special because Joe had told it. And he had told it with clarity of mind and speech. He was healed. There was no doubt.

In the coming weeks they continued to be amazed. It was as though Joseph's, tongue had been unleashed. Like a powerful river which continues to flow underneath a thick surface of ice, now that the chunks of his problem melted under the doctor's care, his mind and tongue gushed forth in torrents of conversation.

He talked of happenings his parents had talked about years before. He told stories they couldn't recall ever having told in his presence. It was a keen reminder to Susannah that listening children are capable of absorbing much more than adults give them credit for.

She pondered all this while her heart sang praises to God for working this miracle in her son's life.

chapter 43

Petitions

The 1920s began with life going on much as usual on the farm. There were hardly any spare moments. The children were growing fast. Taking care of them now differed from when they were younger, but it was no less challenging. In fact, Susannah sometimes thought it more so. With age, their problems seemed to grow more complex.

There was so much she wanted to teach them. So much she wanted to warn them of. The world was changing rapidly, and how could one ever prepare young souls to go forth into the temptations of life, yet remain strong in the face of pressure?

In February of 1921 Susannah's mother died. The letter from Canada with the news came weeks later. Mother. Gone now too. The ache was real for Susannah even though she hadn't known her mother well. Again, questions and memories churned through her brain. She had no doubt that her mother had endured much grief because of circumstances beyond her control. With relief Susannah realized she had nothing against her mother. *I'm just glad she has no more earthly trials to face,* she thought with tears in her eyes. *And I look forward to meeting her in heaven.* Even so, the world seemed a lonely place, just knowing she was gone.

In July of the following year it was John's mother, Nancy Anna, who answered that call from above. At age 71, she had been longing for the past few years to join her husband in eternal joy.

"Now we are the old people," John said softly to Susannah following the burial.

"Ach, ya," Susannah agreed. When had it all happened? Both she and John were nearing their fifties. With both sets of parents gone, the reality couldn't be denied.

"There's still plenty of work for us though," she added. Her thoughts went to their own family.

John nodded.

Mary and Maggie were now young ladies. Mary, the oldest, was a good worker and sturdy. Maggie was more delicate and craved the finer things in life. She did her share of work willingly enough, in spite of her small frame. Amanda was nearly sixteen. She was in demand for helping out at others' homes. Susannah believed it was in part due to her nurturing personality. Enoch was tall for his age and was a great blessing to John in helping around the farm. Joseph, just younger than him, held his own, though Susannah thought she could still detect that he sometimes felt inferior to Enoch. She wished to convince him that in her eyes there were no favorites. Then there were the "little girls." How they disliked that term! Where could one ever find a kinder girl than Nancy? Susannah was so grateful that the rickets she'd suffered from as a baby left few after effects. And Leah. At almost nine years old, she was still so young. Susannah wished to shield her from hard things, but she knew too that she must not be babied. Jacob, had he lived, would be three. How her heart ached to see him again.

Susannah's thoughts pondered each of her family by turn. Such a responsibility. She was sure to fail, and had done so many times already. If only, by God's grace, the family could turn out to be honorable, God-fearing adults, worthy of the trust of those about them, then maybe she could feel they'd done their duty.

Her only other hope was that life would be kind to them. And if that was too much to ask, then please, Lord, let them become better, not bitter, through their circumstances. For it was certain no father or mother could forever shield their children.

Susannah shuddered as an incident of several days ago popped into her mind.

It had begun with a gypsy woman knocking at the kitchen door. That wasn't so unusual, as groups of these vagabonds camped on the Susquehanna riverbanks. Their wanderings often took them into the neighboring hills and trails, and it was not unheard of for one of them to come to the door. But it was enough to make one nervous. It was common knowledge that these people didn't like to work and seldom held jobs for any length of time. At the same time, their large clans needed to eat. Apparently knocking on a farmhouse door and asking for food was easier than working for it.

Sometimes they came up to a house in pairs. One would come to the door in pretense of asking for some small favor while the accomplice would be busy outdoors in a barn or outbuilding. Later, the family would discover missing items. But the visitors were so stealthy that one never actually saw them in the act. Only after the distraction was over did one realize what had occurred.

Susannah looked sharply right and left past the gaudily dressed woman on her steps that day. She couldn't detect the presence of anyone else. Finally she focused on the dark-haired visitor.

"What can I do for you?" she asked warily. She was aware that Nancy and Leah were close behind her. These wandering strangers held great fascination for the girls.

"I'm selling fabric today," was the reply. She reached into the depths of a large bag slung across her shoulder. With a flash of bright bracelets she held out a handful of yard goods in front of Susannah's face.

"There's more in the bag. Let me come in, and I'll show you."

Before Susannah quite knew how, the woman had brushed past her and into the kitchen. Susannah and the girls followed close behind.

Chattering a steady stream in a heavy accent, the gypsy spread out her bright, large-print fabric on the table.

Susannah's heart sank. None of it was suitable for their plain Mennonite clothes. How could she refuse to buy, yet still get this bold stranger out of her home?

"You can pay me with food if you wish," came the woman's offer. No doubt she thought lack of money was the reason Susannah hesitated.

Never having learned the art of useless words, Susannah said honestly, "I can't use any of those colors. We don't wear flashy clothes."

The dark eyes narrowed to slits. "Nothing?" she asked tonelessly. "Not even this?" She held up a bright blue piece with large white dots.

Susannah shook her head. She gestured to her own plain dress, then at the girls'.

The peddler's eyes glittered.

Quickly Susannah reached behind herself to the bowl of fresh eggs the children had gathered that morning.

"Here, take these." While the woman watched she placed the eggs carefully into the gypsy's sack.

With a sniff, the lady gathered her gaudy fabrics together and stuffed them into the sack as well.

Turning to leave, she acted as though seeing the girls for the first time. Muttering something Susannah couldn't understand, she gave both Nancy and Leah long, cold stares.

It was what she did next that chilled Susannah to the bone, in spite of the warm summer day.

The gypsy lifted her hand to her mouth and spat onto her fingers. Reaching out toward the wide-eyed girl, she touched Nancy's apron-clad shoulder and chanted some words in monotone.

Then she glared at Susannah and said, "This girl will have an awful life!" With a rustle of her flowing skirt, she swept from the kitchen and out the door.

Susannah shuddered as she watched her leave.

"What did she mean, Mother?" Nancy asked breathlessly.

"Ach! Just trying to scare us. She wants us to believe she can put a hex on you." Susannah tried to sound calm.

"We don't believe in such things, girls. It's not something to worry

204

about. Now go back to your work."

Still looking bewildered, Nancy turned to go.

"Wait." Susannah had an idea. "Let's wash your apron though." Deftly she slipped the long apron from Nancy's shoulders. "Now go." She gave her daughter a gentle push and a crooked smile.

Now, days later, the memory of that bold woman in her kitchen still made her shiver. It was common knowledge that the gypsies practiced witchcraft, but until now Susannah hadn't seen it performed. If she didn't know better, it would scare her even more. But, thankfully, the power of darkness was powerless in a Christian life. She paused again to thank her Lord for that. And to ask Him to protect her children.

chapter 44

Oh, Maggie

The winter of 1923 stretched on and on. The Pennsylvania locals thought it was a hard one, but to John and Susannah, who were used to winters in Ontario and Iowa, it wasn't unusually so. One must simply dress in layers of clothing and not go outside for anything other than necessities.

At last it relented, as winters always must when the daylight hours lengthen and the sun's rays strengthen. The frost, however, wasn't out of the ground yet, and John's field work hadn't begun.

One Saturday afternoon he had a suggestion for his wife. "Shall we go visiting, Susannah?"

"To whom?" she asked.

"I'm thinking of Abs Tharps," John replied. "They're getting up in years and can't get out much anymore."

"Oh, that would be nice. Yes, I'll go along," Susannah agreed. The Tharps had blessed them in the past. A visit to cheer them was the least they could do in return.

Besides, with the long, cold days of winter now behind them, it would be good to get some fresh air. Being cooped up in the house with several young adults had been stressful for Susannah this winter.

Maggie had been especially moody lately. Susannah didn't know what her trouble was. Upon questioning her, all she received was vague answers. She'd decided to drop it. Maybe it was Maggie's conscience nagging her in the matter of accepting Christ and taking up baptism. If that were the case, Susannah didn't want to meddle. Maggie must make up her own mind. And when she was ready to talk, then she would be there for her.

So it was with anticipation for a pleasant outing that Susannah donned her light shawl and climbed to the wagon seat beside John.

The March breeze was pleasant. It held a touch of both the chill of the winter behind them and a promise of warmer days to come. The creek babbled cheerily over its bed of rocks, ever tumbling towards the river. Tree limbs stretched out boughs with swollen tips.

A visit with a shut-in often has the strange effect of being as much a blessing to the ones visiting as the visited. This was the case today. Hours later John and Susannah turned the team toward home. The sun was lowering itself toward the hills and shadows stretched across the dirt road. The former warm breeze now felt chilly, but Susannah scarcely noticed. Her heart was warmed by the afternoon. John was in a talkative mood, and they discussed trivial community matters as the horse plodded in the direction of their farm.

"I hope the girls started supper," Susannah mentioned as they turned in their lane. "I told Maggie to go ahead. Nancy and Leah can help her."

"No doubt they did, then," was John's calm reply as his wife got off the wagon seat and headed up the walkway.

This wasn't the case, however.

When Susannah entered the house there was no sign of any preparations of the evening meal. Nancy and Leah sat stiffly at the table, with strange, wide-eyed looks.

"What's wrong?" asked Susannah.

Neither girl answered.

"Where's Maggie?" Susannah asked next.

"She's not home," Nancy said slowly.

"Not home?" Susannah was puzzled. Maggie hadn't mentioned any plans for the afternoon. But then, Maggie hadn't mentioned much of anything lately. A strange foreboding gripped her heart. "Where is she?" she asked.

By now John had unhitched the horse. As he entered the kitchen for a drink, he met the startled gaze of his wife. Then he looked at Nancy and Leah. "Something wrong?" he asked.

"Maggie left." This time Leah spoke.

"Well, she'll probably be back soon, won't she? Have you started supper for Mother?" John wasn't perturbed.

The girls exchanged glances. Apparently supper was far from their minds.

"She said she's leaving, and not to worry," Nancy volunteered in an expressionless tone. "She left with the mailman."

"The mailman! Ralph Ulsh?"

Both girls nodded.

Now their parents exchanged glances. This didn't make sense.

"I think she left to marry him," Leah said bluntly.

John looked as if someone had hit him in the stomach.

"Are you sure she didn't just go to do some work for him?" John asked as they struggled to piece together this weird information.

Both girls promptly shook their heads.

"I'm going to hitch up the horse, Susannah. Get the lantern ready for me. Nancy can go with me. We'll go bring her back. Leah, you stay here with Mother," he said more softly, noticing her pale features.

Mechanically Susannah filled the lantern with oil. John would need it. Dusk was nearly here, and by the time he got down to Port Trevorton, it would be dark.

"Nancy, dress warmly," she admonished. "It will be chilly down by the river." With this she handed the lantern to Nancy and urged her out the door.

From inside the window she watched John and Nancy go out the lane. *Surely they'll come back in a few hours with Maggie,* she consoled herself. All the same, fear clutched her heart. It threatened to choke her.

What had come over Maggie? Why hadn't she been willing to talk?

Ralph Ulsh, indeed! The very idea! John would no doubt give the lass a stern lecture on their way home. Where had they failed with Maggie that she'd even consider such a thing?

Like heavy cream in a churn, Susannah's fears and questions tumbled over each other. In a daze she stoked the fire against the chill of night.

Why not make potato soup? We have to eat, and John deserves a hot supper when he gets home. She sent Leah to the cellar with a bowl to get potatoes.

"There aren't many nice ones there anymore," Leah stated when she returned. To prove her point she gestured to the wrinkly, sprouting tubers in the bowl.

"Ach, yes," Susannah agreed. "Soon it'll be time to cut those up and plant them. We'll just use the best ones in the meantime."

She busied herself helping Leah with the tedious job. Leah was unusually quiet. Perhaps she was lost in her own perplexities of her sister's actions.

Setting the pot of potatoes on to cook, Susannah then placed the peelings in another pot to boil. The chickens would devour the warm mash of peelings.

Once these ordinary chores were done and the kitchen lantern lit, there was nothing left to distract her. She wanted so badly to be calm, yet her nerves were as taut as a loaded clothesline. Aimlessly she wandered about the kitchen, peering frequently out the window, looking at the darkness, and willing a lantern glow and a team into view—a wagon with three figures on the seat. Why not? Once John set out upon a task there wasn't much that stopped him. So why worry?

But worry she did. Several times she attempted to line up her thoughts into prayer, but it didn't work. They remained in such a tangle that she couldn't form a sensible prayer out of them.

"Here comes Father." It was Leah who spotted them first.

Susannah rushed to open the door, with Leah on her heels.

Words failed her. Only John and Nancy entered the dimly lit kitchen. John's face was as pale as when he'd been deathly sick with pneumonia.

"We were too late." His voice was heavy with defeat. "They were married this afternoon."

chapter 45

Grief

John's words settled on her ears, but not into her heart. "Maggie? Married? Today?" All she could get out were single word questions. "Ya." John sighed heavily. "When we got to Ralph's house, I sent Nancy in to fetch her. She wouldn't come out. Said she's not coming home. That she's a married woman now. Right, Nancy?"

Nancy nodded solemnly.

Susannah groaned. Thoughts tumbled over themselves in her brain. It didn't make sense. Maggie. Their second daughter. The first of the children to marry—if this hasty arrangement could be called a marriage. Ralph Ulsh. The man's name was familiar. But to think of him as a son-in-law would take a miracle. He must be in his thirties, and Maggie was only nineteen. It wasn't that the Ulshs were bad people. They were local neighbors who had been in the area for years. Quite well-to-do people, in fact. But they weren't Mennonite. Or plain at all. Why, Ralph's wife, Mabel, had just died not so long ago. How many children did he have anyhow? It had been news at the time it happened, but right now Susannah couldn't remember. He probably needed someone to care for his family, and Maggie had fallen for it.

Why hadn't they seen this coming? Had she really been so blind?

Maggie had been unusually interested in fetching the mail the last while. That must be it. Had she been meeting Ralph all the time? And planning this?

Maggie had always been the most ladylike of their daughters. Her looks were above average. No doubt Ralph noticed all this too. Oh, had this really been going on right under her own nose?

John had by now taken a chair by the stove and sat dejectedly, head in his hands.

"What did we do wrong?" he asked, anguish in his voice. The question tore deeply at Susannah's heart.

"If only I knew," she answered in a moan. They'd had such high hopes for their family. Now this.

"We must pray," he decided. Rising, he walked unsteadily to the living room settee.

Susannah joined him there. John knelt, as if in a trance. So did she. She waited for him to begin.

His first words came out hoarsely. "Our Father in heaven."

Susannah waited for more.

No more words came from her husband. Instead he sobbed—deep, gasping sobs that came from deep in his chest.

Susannah's tears joined in. They knelt side by side, bathing the settee with tears that felt as though they would flow forever.

The next few days were dark and sad. They met again with Maggie, but it was as though Maggie had turned into a stranger overnight. She had indeed eloped with the widower, Ralph Ulsh. She was done being plain and poor. Especially poor. Ralph had promised her a fine new home in the future. And as many pretty dresses as she wanted. He said she wouldn't have to be a slave to her family anymore.

John and Susannah bore the saucy tirade for a while, then John spoke up. "What about your soul, Maggie?" he pleaded. "Worldly things and pretty things can never replace peace for your soul."

Maggie tossed her head impatiently. "I can always come back to the church when I'm old," she said. "For now, I'll go to Ralph's church with him. Things don't have to be so up and down plain. It's time I got some fresh air."

"But you don't believe like he does." Susannah couldn't help herself. "How can you share life with someone who was raised so differently? Why, he's a Christian Scientist, isn't he?"

Maggie paused. "Yes, he is. I mean, *we* are. And if you really love someone, what is so bad about believing differently. Love makes up for all that, you know."

Her flippant answers brought fresh tears to her parents' cheeks.

"Don't worry about me. I'm happy now," she insisted.

Further pleading did no good. She was now Mrs. Ulsh. She would enjoy this exciting new life. If they wouldn't rejoice with her, that wasn't her problem.

The miracle of spring went largely unnoticed at the Brubaker home that year. It was as though Maggie's choice blighted all the fresh, new life that sprang forth in the clear, warm sunshine.

Grief, Susannah decided, didn't always come in the form of death. What she had experienced while losing little Jacob now paled in comparison with their daughter's waywardness. This time the grief was directed at her own failure as a parent. With the sick baby, she had recognized it as the hand of God, but with Maggie she felt responsible.

Maggie's decision was made. There was no changing it now. Marriage vows weren't meant to be broken. Susannah knew it was done and final, but that didn't stop her thoughts. What could she have done differently? Why had she failed to see what was coming?

On top of it all was the nagging fear of what others were saying. The elopement caused no small stir in the community. Tongues would wag, cluck, and tsk, tsk. Susannah could imagine it all so well. What might the Ulsh clan be thinking and saying among themselves? Did they think Maggie had enticed Ralph? That she'd made a smart move to better herself? Did they, perhaps, feel that Ralph had now married beneath himself by taking a poor Mennonite girl as his second wife?

The Ulshs had every right to feel like that, for they were good citizens, and Susannah knew she must not harbor resentment. No, it was Maggie's foolishness. Or her own, as her mother. And it was for life. Time was the only thing that would show them how things would turn out. But even if Maggie did come to her senses, it might be too late to change from her worldly stand and come back to the church.

"It's not too late to pray," John said to his wife one day. "For our other children, at least." Accepting their daughter's choice deeply grieved him as well. Though Maggie had never publicly stated her belief in the Lord or become a baptized member of the Mennonite church, it still felt like a betrayal. A betrayal of all they had tried to teach their family. John too was haunted by questions of what they might have done differently.

The shadow of all this hadn't yet lifted when their oldest, Mary, announced her own wedding plans.

On June 6, 1923, Mary was united in marriage to Ammon Parker. Mary was twenty-one, and old enough to make her own decisions, her parents conceded.

Two girls married and gone in such a short time. It seemed like yesterday to Susannah that they were born. How their arrival had changed her life! And now they were gone already. Her musings turned inward again. Had she taught them enough? Yes, they knew how to work. But had she taught them enough of what it meant to walk side by side with their partners through anything God might send them? To trust God when all looked impossible? To be strong when the other was sick? To be kind, patient, and loving? To make do with what income there was? And if there were children, to raise them in the fear of the Lord?

Susannah felt her own inadequacy keenly. She still had much to learn. Especially in areas of trusting the Lord when things made no sense.

Her next plea was for continued wisdom for herself. Wisdom and faith. Both for herself and her married daughters.

chapter 46

Life Continues

A year later, in August, life dealt a cruel blow to Maggie. She and Ralph became parents of a tiny baby. It was an infant much anticipated on Maggie's part. This baby would unite Ralph and herself. It would make their union complete. Yes, she cared for Ralph's other children, but she longed for a family of her own. Hers and Ralph's.

There were problems. Serious ones. And the baby lived less than a day. Maggie's grief was real and raw. John and Susannah grieved too. It was their first grandchild, and God had chosen to take it to heaven so soon. They feared for Maggie. She was still so young and had always been so slight and delicate. How would she handle this? Would she rely on the Lord for strength?

"Maybe this will draw her closer to the Lord," John mentioned as he and Susannah discussed the death.

"It's probably her first real taste of living like a Christian Scientist," Susannah mused. "They don't believe in using medicines or doctors. So I've heard anyway. Oh, it's so different from how we raised her!"

Both were silent, pondering the situation. It was out of their hands. Whether or not a doctor could have saved the infant's life, they would never know. The big thing to be thankful for was that Maggie's own life had been spared. For this, her parents praised God. It was one more reason to keep praying for Maggie.

Amanda was now the oldest at home. She had matured greatly since her two older sisters were gone. She was of the age when the young folks attended youth gatherings and crowds. Young people from the entire community might attend those crowds. This meant a mingling of youth who were both Mennonite and non-Mennonite.

John and Susannah weren't blind to Amanda's charm. It gained the young girl many a friend among the youth. Her parents didn't approve of some of those "friends."

What could they do? They prayed for wisdom and guidance. Amanda felt their concerns, but wasn't too worried until they made a decision on her behalf. Then it was met with emotional squalls.

They had learned a bitter lesson with Maggie. Not wanting to risk another daughter to a worldly future, John and Susannah arranged to send Amanda to the Lancaster/Ephrata church district. That area had a youth group made up of mostly Mennonite youth. Perhaps if they got Amanda settled in a stable community, it would be better.

"But I like my friends!" Amanda protested. "I'm happy here."

It was a time of distress for both parents and daughter. John and Susannah remained firm. By now they knew parenting wasn't smooth sailing.

At last Amanda gave in. Somewhat reluctantly she packed for the trip to Lancaster, but Susannah thought she detected a spark of interest in the prospect of what might prove an adventure. She prayed Amanda would in time realize the plan was meant for her good, and that it wouldn't drive a wedge of resentment between their daughter and themselves.

Having Amanda gone from their home meant they would have to trust God to protect her and provide for her. Although plans for boarding and a job had been made, those weren't the biggest concerns for the mother heart. There were countless "what-ifs" that begged for mental attention. What if they were merely freeing Amanda to do the very thing they wished to prevent? What if she got involved in something they disapproved of and they weren't there to intervene?

The move proved to be a bumpy one. Amanda got settled in Ephrata and liked her work, but she was often homesick. This caused a burden of guilt for Susannah. Had they done the right thing? Or were they now to be haunted by the fact that they'd caused Amanda undue anxiety?

"We must just trust that we did what was best for her," John told Susannah. "And that in the long run, she'll see too that it was for her own good."

Ever since the Great War had ended, it seemed the world was a different place. Women who had mostly worked at home were now in demand to work in factories and businesses. While the men had been off to war, the women had filled in at positions never thought fitting for them. They had exercised their work skills and management and had proved capable in every way. Now they wanted more, and the opportunities were there. And if that wasn't enough, they also wanted the right to vote. What would they think of next?

The horrors of war had ushered in an attitude of anything-goes. Fashions such as one had never dreamed of showed up in clothes and hairstyles. Rural populations shifted from farm life to city setting in quest of fun and entertainment.

One heard much about Boy Scouts these days. Not to be left behind, there was soon a similar Girl Scouts. It seemed they taught valuable lessons to those children who were now removed from the previous generation who had learned those same skills at home from parents.

The government was making strides to gain back the financial losses caused by the war, but European countries remained crippled by the destruction on their own soil. There was a general air of unrest. What was to come next?

June of 1926 brought a robust son to live with Ammon and Mary Parker. They named him Paul. Now the reality of being grandparents set in for John and Susannah.

Two years later, in 1928, Amanda married a young man named Paul Landis. It was with relief that her parents received the news. Paul was of the Mennonite faith. They had high hopes that he and Amanda would share a strong union and provide a godly home should God

217

send them children.

Amanda and her young husband's goal of soon acquiring a home of their own proved to be a real challenge. In 1929 the financial bottom fell out of many businesses and banks. Hardship descended upon thousands who were suddenly out of work. It became a serious challenge for these unemployed masses to find enough food to feed their families.

For the people in rural areas and on farms it wasn't an immediate crisis. Farm work continued as it had before. There was seedtime and harvest, and the cows had to be milked daily. Cream was churned into butter, eggs gathered, and gardens tended. There was no lack of food for those on farms. Their hardship came when they could no longer sell their excess products to city dwellers who were out of work and money. This in turn cut the cash flow for farmers. Thus, the crisis was felt by everyone.

John and Susannah, though concerned, were not unduly alarmed, as hardship had been their lifelong companion. Though they had never faced starvation, both of them knew what it was like to eat less than one might desire.

This new turn of events seemed to be just a continuation of the lifestyle they were familiar with. It was the younger generation accustomed to greater ease and abundant food who were most devastated.

The orchard John had dreamed of and toiled over for so long finally began to bear fruit. With great joy Susannah set a fresh cherry pie on the table one day for her family. Cutting a generous slice for John first, she cut the rest for the children. Finally she took a piece for herself.

It was a pleasure to watch John savor the oozy tartness of the treat. Slowly he chewed, then spit the pits neatly on a pile beside his plate.

"Why do you leave the pits in, Mother?" Enoch asked.

"It takes fewer cherries to fill the pie that way," Susannah responded automatically.

"Oh," was all Enoch said. He was busy eating his pie.

"If you had waited as long as we have for fresh fruit, you wouldn't waste any either," John said, coming to Susannah's defense. He gave his wife a contented smile before taking a big swallow of milk.

chapter 47

Hard Times

Community life for the Mennonites was a large part of life itself. This didn't change with the onset of the Depression. There were still work bees and building projects for the men. On such days the women might also gather together, to help cook or simply to visit.

The church building that nestled on the hillside by the creek was a gathering place on Sundays for worship. Teams were tied to the trees that dotted the hillside. Now the menfolk of the area decided that a shed should be built to shelter the horses during cold weather while the members were indoors at the service.

Discussions on this topic followed. A neighbor offered to let the brethren harvest trees from his woodland for the needed lumber. That taken care of, a collection was taken up for the tin to put on the roof of their pole-type structure.

Plans progressed quickly. Trees were felled, and by working together it wasn't long before the men had raised the framework and put siding on the shed. Their order of tin was delivered to the site.

John lived only a short distance from the church, so he was able to be there almost every day when the men gathered there to work.

Roofing day dawned clear and sunny. In good spirits, the men clambered upon the framework. Soon the ring of hammers on the new tin echoed from the hillside.

John, ever precise, had taken the measurements for the needed tin, so when one of the men informed him that they were running short, he was surprised.

"Hmmm," he said slowly. His first thought was that one of the young men might have hidden some as a prank. Carefully he checked his calculations. By now the hammering on the roof had ceased. Men remeasured the roof and counted the sheets already on. Then they counted the few left on the pile. They came up short.

John felt as if all the men were eyeing him. It must have been his mistake. He had taken charge of the order, after all.

"I felt sure we had the right amount. We counted it carefully when we unloaded, didn't we, Enoch?"

His son, who had also been involved with the building project, nodded.

"It must have been a prank, then," said one of the men.

"Guess we'll have to scout around to see if we can find it," offered another.

"Hey!" came an excited shout from a young man still up on the roof. "Look over there!"

All eyes turned to see where he pointed.

Neighbor Rolland Bierly's home was in full view, with the porch facing uphill toward the church house. Nailed on at a rakish angle, glinting in the morning sun, was a piece of new tin on the roof of Rol's porch.

The puzzle of the missing tin was solved. But now what?

Several of the men chuckled. Rol was no dummy, though he had the reputation of being the neighborhood drunk. Any money he honestly earned was soon squandered on the drink he was enslaved to.

All the men were certain he hadn't spent money for that new tin. Not in these hard times. And not when a pile of it lay right there practically under his nose next door in the churchyard.

"He didn't even cut it to size!" exclaimed one man.

Indeed the tin hung down far over the roof edge. Rol hadn't thought it necessary to bother trimming it.

"Shall we go get it?" someone asked. "He can't deny where it came from! Then we can finish up here and go home"

John shook his head. "No, let him have it. I'll order some more to finish this."

"But we paid for it!" someone protested.

"I'll pay for the extra." John was firm.

Several others agreed with John. It was best not to meddle with Bierly. When he was sober, he was a nice enough man, but when drunk, no one wished to raise his ire. Besides, maybe this way he could see what a church was for—to work together and to show love to one's neighbor, even a thief. Jesus would have tolerated the problem, even turned His other cheek. They would do the same. Maybe the man's conscience would prick him yet.

The group dispersed. Men went home for the day, It would no doubt be an interesting topic at many tables that evening.

John walked home slowly. His way led right past the Bierly house. It was the same house he and Susannah had moved to when they first left the Tharps after moving here to Snyder County.

They were neighbors. Susannah felt sorry for Mrs. Bierly. She had spoken of it often. But there wasn't much one could do about the situation except send food. That way Rol couldn't waste it on his alcohol.

This wasn't the first time the Brubakers had to deal with their unconverted neighbors. One morning during chore time the children had announced that a dozen chickens were missing from the coop.

John had done a thorough investigation. Seeing no signs of a predator and no blood trail, he was sure the hens had been removed by humans.

"Let it go," had been his advice then too. "Rolland's wife and children must eat. I doubt he supplies much food for the table."

Sure enough, Leah, walking by on an errand a few days later, had seen their own chickens scratching and clucking in the Bierly yard. The watchful eye of Devil, Rolland's black dog, gazed upon his new charges possessively.

For a while all was fine, but then John began to notice that his supply of feed was dwindling amazingly fast—too fast. One morning he counted the bags he kept in the barn, and there was one less than he had counted the evening before. The puzzle piece fell into place. Those new chickens at the neighbors must eat, or quit laying eggs. Why, yes. Why hadn't he thought of it sooner?

Susannah was glad John remained so calm about it all. She herself was aggravated by the boldness. But as John reminded her, what would Mrs. Bierly and the children eat otherwise? But didn't they know other people were struggling to keep food on the table too?

Feeling remorse for her attitude, Susannah sent food up to their neighbors at times. That is, if she could get Nancy or Leah to deliver it. No one liked to enter the Bierlys' yard, or even the driveway, as Devil took his duty as watchdog seriously. One never quite knew when he might come sneaking up from the back and administer a quick snap to the ankle.

Time had by now brought several more grandchildren to the family. Ammon and Mary had a baby daughter, and then a son in 1929.

In the early part of 1930 a little girl was born to Maggie and Ralph. No doubt small Marion Sue would have her mother's complete devotion.

Amanda and Paul also welcomed their first son, named John.

With these changes Susannah was always busy, even if her own family was nearly grown. If there was ever any spare time, one of her married daughters could always use her help.

In 1932 Nancy married Allen Stauffer. That December Enoch married Cathcrine Fox. Two leaving in one year left quite a void.

"They're leaving faster than they came," Susannah commented to John.

"Ach, ya," John replied. "We're getting to be old folks for sure."

Susannah nodded. She pondered life and all the changes that had come their way. God had certainly been with them, although times hadn't always been easy. There were dark threads woven in with the brighter, not unlike the rugs she enjoyed braiding. Looking back, one could see a blend of blessings and trials. The pattern had at times taken unplanned pathways. What she did not know was that more dark threads were still to come.

chapter 48

A New Calling

The year of 1933 was packed with events that altered the community. In May there was the wedding of the community's widower bishop, John Stauffer. His wife of choice this time was Mary Bauman, a 49-year-old single lady. This caused no small stir in the area.

No sooner had this event cooled when another occurred not three months later. An accident along the trail left Bishop John dead, and Mary now his widow.

Not only did this arouse sympathy for his children and for Mary, it also brought questions. How was the community to function without a bishop? There was no deacon either, since the elderly Elias Bauman had passed away several years ago.

Susannah's heart ached for Mary. They had known each other in Iowa already. Mary was only nine years younger than herself. If ever there was a kind, gentle woman, it was Mary. These drastic events of late must have left Mary's world spinning like a top out of control.

Since Bishop John had presided over the Lancaster/Ephrata area as well as here in Snyder County, his death left a large void. Church council decided a new bishop would be ordained in Ephrata this time. Lots were cast, and the chosen man was Jacob S. Stauffer. His duty was now also to preside over both districts.

Church council also addressed the need for another minister here in Snyder County. There was to be an ordination in November, followed by an ordination for a deacon the following spring.

No one was more surprised to find himself in the lot for the minister's ordination than Susannah's husband, John. He voiced his surprise and doubts to Susannah on the afternoon of the day the votes were taken.

"There are others who could do a better job. I'm not much of a talker. You know that. And I'm up in age already!"

Susannah had no ready answer. She knew his protests were true, but she also knew her husband's heart was gentle and kind. Though he wasn't perfect, she knew he tried to live as best he could according to Jesus' example and the Word of God. He wasn't one to quickly fall for any new thing that came along. Yes, he was 58. Would he be able to deal with the mental and emotional turmoil that was sure to be a part of a minister's life? His health had never been strong after his severe bout with heat stroke and pneumonia.

"We must wait and see what God decides," she finally said. "He won't make a mistake." Though she had always said this, did she really believe it? In her own mind, she thought John was right. Probably one of the other men would be better suited to the minister's duty. Surely God saw that as well. They would have to wait until ordination day to see which one God chose. Once again there was no one else to turn to but their heavenly Father.

The November day of the ordination was as gray as their spirits. Clouds sagged low enough to scuff the hilltops. One could nearly touch them. A chilly mist rose from the creek that tumbled through the churchyard. The new sheds were packed full of teams. A few were tied to trees here and there, because the sheds were full.

Bishop Jacob and Deacon Levi from Ephrata had come to oversee the ceremony. Jacob's duty was to lead the service, but the choosing was to be God's.

There was hardly any visiting prior to the service. The day's outcome was too serious for that.

Susannah took her place on the front bench on the women's side, along with the wives of the other candidates. She felt conspicuously out of place. How must John feel?

A glance showed him seated calmly, head bowed, hands folded in his lap.

The opening sermon was powerful. They were reminded of the need for another minister, but also that God's choosing wasn't always the way men would choose. Despite his protests of inability, God had chosen Moses in the Old Testament to lead Israel out of Egypt. Hadn't God also chosen David, the youngest and least likely of all Jesse's sons? And they were reminded that when God chose, He also supplied the ability.

Finally it was time. Finally, or already, Susannah couldn't tell. Deacon Levi and another man took the same number of hymnals to the counsel room as there were men in the lot. Only one hymnal contained a piece of paper with the verse Proverbs 16:33 written on it in German. "The lot is cast into the lap; but the whole disposing thereof is of the Lord."

In the privacy of that room the songbooks were shuffled until no human knew which one contained the paper. They were then returned to the main room of the church and solemnly arranged in a row on the simple pulpit.

At the bishop's direction, each man in the lot rose to take one of the books and then sat down again.

Susannah dared not watch. She hardly dared breathe. The silence in the congregation could nearly be felt.

Jacob stepped out to approach the men. In these last few minutes they were still all bearing the load, but within seconds that would change. Only one would be chosen. One's life would forever change. The others would be free to resume a normal life.

In the silence Susannah heard Jacob rustle the pages of a hymnal. The sound was loud in the tense atmosphere.

It seemed like hours later when Jacob's husky voice announced, "God hath not spared you."

Did she dare raise her eyes to see to whom this was spoken? What she saw were men handing back their hymnals to the bishop. What did that mean? John sat there clutching his with a white-knuckled grip. John? Her John? Disbelief slowly registered in her mind. John, the new minister?

Jacob returned the hymnals to the pulpit. He then turned to bid his right hand to John, and asked him to rise. In a blur, Susannah noted all this. The two men exchanged the kiss of peace. Jacob continued to encourage John and recited the words customary for an ordination. Words that announced to John and the entire congregation what his duties were. The German words weren't unfamiliar to Susannah. She'd heard them before at other ordinations—when other men had been chosen. This time they seemed as leaden as the gray clouds outdoors.

With the service over, a parting hymn was chosen and begun. Vaguely Susannah was aware of all this swirling around her. What must John be thinking? What could she do to help him? What did a minister's wife need to know or do, anyhow? She, a minister's wife? She couldn't wrap her mind around the brand-new truth.

Numbly she received the greetings and encouragement offered to her by the other women after the service. It was too much. She only wished to be in private somewhere. Away from all these people. Away from the curious looks and whispers that rustled about the edges of the group.

Finally it was time to go. The distance home was way too short today. It was made in near silence. Susannah, who had wished to be home just minutes before, now wished they could just keep going. Going somewhere. Anywhere but home right now. Home, where they must face this new reality.

John's face appeared calm, but Susannah knew him well enough to know his mind was probably not. He would need time to adjust to this new weight of responsibility, and to brace up for the duty of rising in front of the congregation with a sermon to deliver.

Susannah suddenly felt selfish. John would have a struggle ahead. Why was *she* feeling so burdened?

The truth stared back at her. Because she loved him. Any burden that was his was also hers. It was a part of sharing life. A wordless prayer rose from her heart. A prayer for wisdom and strength for John in this new stage of their lives. And for herself, to be what John would need from her in the coming days. Whatever that might be.

chapter 49

Unrest

Gradually the grip of the Depression eased its clawlike hold upon the United States. The country's new president, Franklin D. Roosevelt, faced mountains of challenges, including massive unemployment, collapsed stock markets, thousands of closed banks, and agriculture prices that had fallen below the cost of production.

On top of that, President Roosevelt had been a victim of polio in his younger years. The disease had left him with some physical limitations, but these he masked with a cheerful demeanor and an optimistic approach. His beginning at the White House promised a "new deal" for the American people.

John, however, didn't begin his service in the ministry with any high hopes of ambitious reform. As Susannah had expected, he struggled mightily with his new role. Though she was pleased with his efforts and the messages he brought forth from God's Word, she realized he had been right—he would probably never be a fluent speaker. He simply spoke the truth in a simple, straightforward way. It wasn't his gift to add a lot of powerful word illustrations. "I can't hold them spellbound in awe," he confided to Susannah one day.

"You're doing the best you can," she reassured him truthfully. "God knows that too."

"When I think of all my own failures, I can hardly preach at all," he shared with her. "Especially when I think of Maggie…" He lapsed into silence. "When I think of how we failed by her, I feel like a dunce up there. How can I instruct others? I wonder why one of the others wasn't chosen instead of me."

Susannah knew his burdens came from the depths of his heart. How could she help him accept the truth that God had chosen him in spite of the human failings that loomed so large in his own eyes?

Nearly a year after her father's ordination, daughter Leah married Elmer Groff. Susannah would miss her keenly. It was one more reminder that she and John were no longer young. Now Joseph was the only one of their children who wasn't married.

Time added more grandchildren to their family circle. Each of the children's families was growing. There was no lack of joy as these tiny souls entered each home. Though each one also added to the workload, it gave plenty of opportunity for Susannah to help out with the married children's needs. It warmed her heart to see each family grow in faith even as the families grew.

Another heavy cloud of grief soon descended on Ralph and Maggie's life. At five years old, their little Marion Sue died after a brief illness.

This pained John and Susannah as well. They could offer no easy answers to their distraught daughter. They firmly believed the truth in Proverbs chapter 13 which stated that, "The way of transgressors is hard." Maggie had chosen to embrace the faith of Christian Scientists, along with her husband. That their belief didn't accept medical help, even for sick children, was nearly more than Susannah could bear. How could Maggie, ever gentle and ladylike, bear to see her child suffer and die when a doctor could very possibly have saved her?

It was a grief that nearly consumed their daughter again. And a bitter pill for her grandparents as well. Again it was John's calm wisdom that balanced Susannah's more impulsive nature.

"We don't know yet how God is going to use the situation," he reasoned. "And even if we don't agree with their choice of faith, maybe it's a test for us as well. Maybe it is to see if we'll respect others' beliefs, as we'd like to have our own respected."

Susannah couldn't argue with that logic. It was true. God had many times before used death to draw His children closer to Himself. Might that be what He was doing again?

In August of that year, 1935, their son Joseph married young Nora Sensenig. Now John and Susannah were alone. That would take some getting used to. Where had the years gone? In the midst of raising the family, with all the weary work that went with it, this day had seemed far off in a foggy future. Suddenly it was upon them. Was all of life to be so full of changes? Susannah sighed unconsciously. She pondered on the years past. How many more changes might yet be on the horizon?

Just as each season of the year adds its own distinctive beauty, Susannah was slowly learning that so did life. Now that they were alone, there was more time to visit with each other. It was also possible to enjoy special treats that they couldn't have afforded while feeding the family.

One such treat that both she and John enjoyed immensely was Limburger cheese. If one of the family chanced to visit from Ephrata, they usually remembered to bring along a chunk of it as a gift.

If the grandchildren were present at the time they cut into it, there was almost always a discussion.

"We want some too," might be the beginning of it.

"Yes, I'll give you some," Susannah told them.

"What smells so rotten? Ugh! It's the cheese! Mommy, it isn't fit to eat anymore."

"Oh, yes, it is," John chimed in. "Here, give me a slice." So saying, he laid a slice on a piece of bread and ate with gusto.

Passing the plate to the youngsters would tempt them again. But none of them could ever get any of it past their nose into their mouth.

Susannah and John ate their sandwiches with a sparkle in their eyes. In wide-eyed disbelief, the children watched their grandparents enjoy the pungent cheese.

"Would you rather have one of these?" Susannah asked, reaching beneath her apron to her pocket. She brought forth a handful of round, pink Canada mints.

"Yes!" Small heads nodded eagerly. Soon they each had a pink mint and ran off to play.

The farmhouse was now shared with son Enoch and his wife Catherine. Their family would no doubt outgrow the shared quarters, but for now, with only John and Susannah left, the house could easily accommodate the two families. It was also handy for Susannah to help out when Catherine was overwhelmed with caring for several small children.

There were always dishes to help with, little girls whose hair needed braiding, or a baby to rock. In turn, the children ran errands for their grandparents.

Maggie's husband, Ralph, was true to his word. He built a fine new home for Maggie. He was a generous son-in-law, in spite of his worldliness. His goodwill even extended to Maggie's siblings. Business at his feed mill in Port Trevorton prospered.

Prosperity was no match for tribulation, however. In 1936 a son was born to them again. Again death called the baby home. Sorrow seemed to be a part of their life, even if they gained financially.

Other clouds hovered closer and closer. One of them was the situation in Europe, where war was once again brewing. Would the United States join in again? Uneasy misgivings filtered into the rural countryside. There were many questions and few answers.

The other cloud was more elusive, but its presence was felt just the same. There was a decided atmosphere of unrest here in the community. Susannah dreaded the outcome. John preferred to remain on the outskirts of any conflict. In Iowa, as a young lay member, he had been able to do so, but now the situation was different. As a minister, he was considered a leader. One to whom others could bring their problems.

Young Deacon Harry Stauffer brought wisdom beyond his years to the ministry. Susannah knew John greatly appreciated Harry's viewpoints and his methods of handling matters. She only wished John and Harry could also work better with the other minister of the community. Phares Stauffer had been in the position longer than either John or Harry. While he had many good points, as well as being a fluent speaker, he wasn't an easy man to negotiate with.

Susannah sighed. Thoughts on this matter always left her feeling melancholy. Had they left Iowa, with all its unrest, only to face it again here in Snyder County? Why were humans so prone to insist on their own way? Would John be forced to sooner or later take a stand against Phares? How would that go over? Would his health take the strain of conflict? Who was right? Rather, *what* was right?

No answers came to her mind, neither did she expect them to. Time had taught her that God revealed His ways when He was ready. Susannah prayed for patience to wait until then.

chapter 50

War

After Japan attacked Pearl Harbor in 1941, President Roosevelt could no longer withstand the pressure. Following that devastating attack, he joined the war with all the force of the American military.

Troops of young men were summoned and shipped overseas. The conflict was dubbed World War I. Again supplies such as gas and kerosene were rationed, as were some foods. People on the home front needed to sacrifice for the needs of the military.

There were hundreds of tearful partings as young men and boys left families and homeland for the sake of the war. Much ado was made over patriotic sacrifices and the glory of it. An undercurrent of fear was present at the same time. Would they ever return home again? Would they be the same if they did? Thousands had never returned from World War I, and many of those who did return came home wounded in body and spirit.

Mennonites who held staunchly to nonresistance were ridiculed. Susannah could understand why. "We enjoy the same freedoms and privileges as all the others," she explained to her family. "We just don't believe in fighting to gain that freedom."

"Yes," John agreed. "We need to suffer wrongdoing rather than fight for our rights. The Christian's kingdom isn't in this world."

Susannah knew he might have more than one situation in mind besides the war. John strongly held to the belief that nonresistance was not only a virtue to be dusted off and practiced in wartime, it must be practiced in the daily Christian walk as well. How thankful Susannah was that he had taught their children this by example.

Paul and Amanda, whose home wasn't far away, had a hired man who tested their beliefs on the subject. The Hermann family lived in a ramshackle home close by. Jack Hermann sometimes hired out as a day laborer when the mood struck him. He sometimes worked for Paul and Amanda, and when he did, his son Woody frequently came along to "help" as well. Items from the Landis farm had a mysterious way of vanishing on the days when young Woody came. It wasn't unusual to see those very items soon thereafter on the Hermann front porch, which was close to the road. It might be a chunk of meat from the smokehouse, canned goods from the cellar, or tools from the shed.

John and Susannah encouraged their daughter and son-in-law to endure the aggravation. Times were hard, after all, with another war in progress. Those on farms generally fared better than those not on farms.

Ralph and Maggie generously offered such a chance to Maggie's younger sister Leah and her husband Elmer. Up to now Leah and Elmer had lived in Denver, Pennsylvania. Elmer had a job in town, and he knew that if he were called to the military he would have to answer. If he were a farmer, he could refuse military duty under the farm deferment agreement.

With their purchase of the Stahl farm, Ralph and Maggie needed someone to do the farmwork and live in the house. An agreement was made. It was an answer to prayer for the young Groff family.

Susannah rejoiced to have her youngest daughter now living back in the neighborhood. It would be a pleasure to become better acquainted with the Groff grandchildren. There was young Ernest, and the twins, Elwood and Eleanor.

Leah too was glad for the opportunity to visit her mother and siblings more often.

One day not long after her busy young family got settled on the farm, she decided to take the children and go visit at her sister Amanda's house for a while.

Elmer was busy, so she hitched his mule to the wagon for the short trip. This was something unfamiliar to Leah, as she had been used to life away from the farm. In Denver, she and the children didn't have far to walk to stores or neighbors. There had been no family within horse and buggy distance, so she couldn't remember exactly how a harness should be buckled in place.

Just how unacquainted she was with the harnessing details was soon clear to Amanda and Susannah, who was also there for the day.

"What is wrong with Elmer's mule?" Amanda asked. The mule in the wagon with Leah and the youngsters was coming up the driveway. But the mule was walking with a strange gait, his head bent at an odd angle to the side.

Susannah went to the window for a look. "You better go out and see if you can help," she directed Amanda. "It looks like something is wrong."

Amanda wiped her hands on her apron and went out.

Susannah didn't hear their conversation, but she saw Amanda quickly unhitch the mule and lead him from the wagon shafts. With a few more swift motions she slid the entire harness off the mule. Soon he was tied to the rail by the barn.

Susannah watched her daughters come toward the house. Amanda was red-faced with laughter. Leah was pink of cheek too, but she wasn't laughing. Susannah waited for an explanation.

"Ach, my!" Amanda exclaimed. "The poor mule was nearly choked! Leah had the harness on backward, with the tail piece around his neck!" She stifled another round of merriment.

Susannah didn't know what she'd expected to hear, but it certainly wasn't this. In spite of Leah's red face, she too had a hearty laugh.

"Well," Leah sputtered. "Elmer was busy, and I didn't want to bother him. And I haven't done it for so long that I forgot how the harness goes on. We have such an old, loose harness anyway." She turned to take care of the twins. "Laugh if you must. But please don't tell Elmer, or I'll never hear the end of it."

"You'll not hear the end of it anyway, sister!" Amanda was still chuckling.

It warmed Susannah's heart to have most of their children and grandchildren close by. The Parker children, the Groffs, the Stauffers, and Enoch's Brubaker offspring would no doubt recall many pleasant cousin playtimes in later years. It was a memory she didn't have of childhood. She wondered if the youngsters knew how nice they had it. Sometimes a shadow crossed her thoughts as she wondered what trials and tragedies life would send to them. It was a blessing to see them playing together now, oblivious of what the future would bring.

chapter 51

Moving On

Susannah knew she needed to bake something. Not only was the cupboard bare, but somehow the process of baking was soothing to her. It was a comfort to her mind to know that a certain amount of the right ingredients mixed together would produce predictable results. How she wished life were the same!

If life were like baking, you could expect the results to be normal and pleasant. But in life you didn't have that assurance. You might pray as you ought, live as best you knew how, and treat others with more respect than you believed they deserved, and yet the results might be disastrous.

That was the case now. Community goodwill had nearly dissolved. Matters had reached a head, and like the ugly sore of a boil on one's skin, had erupted in a church split. John could hardly talk of it. The grief of it was almost more than he could deal with. He had done all he could to restore peace among the ministry and brethren. So had several others. With advice from the Ephrata ministry, he and Harry had labored with the congregation until they were exhausted, but it was all to no avail. People's minds were set, and they couldn't agree on trivial matters, let alone solid truths.

Minister Phares and his followers now held services on their own, apart from the few families who had remained under the counsel of the Stauffer Mennonite group in Ephrata.

Just this morning John had mentioned the matter again over their simple breakfast.

"What are the young people to do?" His tone was heavy with concern. "If we adults can't come to peaceful agreements, how can they see that the church has anything better to offer than the world? Do they see the love of Christ in us, or just more of what's out in the world—wars and fightings?"

Susannah had no answers. But it was then that she decided she would bake something. John always enjoyed baked goods with his cup of coffee. And that was something she could do something about.

"A spice cake," she decided aloud. "That's what I'll bake. Those don't take sugar." Cooks had to be creative these days because of wartime rationing. Molasses could sometimes be substituted, and this worked well in her spice cake. The grandchildren liked them too. This thought made Susannah smile. Maybe she could also bake a pie with those last ground-cherries from the garden. John would like that.

❋ ❋

Relations in the community remained brittle. Those on the other side of the split wanted no part of reconciliation.

Some of the remaining group wanted to relocate. They believed that would be better than risking the high price of raising children in a setting of confusion and tension.

The matter was taken to counsel in the Ephrata church. After much prayer, a decision was made. If those families who wished to remain under the Stauffer church could reach a unanimous agreement to relocate, they had the blessing of the church to do so.

There was a new branch of Stauffer Mennonites starting up in St. Mary's County, Maryland. After much discussion, it was decided that they would make the move and join that settlement.

So now, at nearly 70 years old, Susannah and John were once more planning a move to a new home. Susannah fervently prayed for the necessary strength to do all the work that went with moving. Her mind was nearly dizzy after months of meetings, planning, and trips to Maryland to locate new homes. The war still going on did not simplify matters. They were moving closer to the nation's capital, and she wondered if that was a wise thing to do in wartime. What if the enemy targeted Washington D.C.? Would a group of plain, nonresistant people be able to make a living there?

Questions pecked at her mind like a flock of chickens searching for grain.

There was a sense of quiet peace about their plans though. Susannah wondered if it was because they had tried so hard to remain in the Lord's will during all this strife? Whatever the reason, she welcomed the halo of tranquility that bathed this new move they needed to make. Would their plans for moving have proceeded as well without the blessing from God? How else could the plans of six families to move to another state have transpired as seamlessly as they had?

But, oh, the changes once more! Enoch and his family would also move to Maryland. For this Susannah was grateful. Paul and Amanda's family would move to Lancaster County, where Paul had been raised. Elmer and Leah also planned to return there as soon as the war ended. Joe and Nora had settled in Berks County when they married. Ammon and Mary Parker would remain in Snyder County, along with Ralph and Maggie Ulsh.

How the partings of family and familiar, everyday things tore at Susannah's heart! How many times had she experienced the upheaval of moving in her years? She mentally added the total. From the Martin household to Betsy's home. Though that she had done only too gladly. Then to Iowa with her brand-new husband. That had taken faith. Then from Emmanuel's shed to their own new home on the prairie. From there to these Snyder County hills. After that, a few shufflings from home to home. It seemed each time just as they got settled in right, it was time to uproot and relocate. *Ach, if it wasn't for this awful situation in the church, I'd be happy to stay right here*, Susannah thought. Was the quest for peace always to come at such a high cost?

"But really," she thought aloud now. "Didn't we always feel confident that we were in God's will when we moved? Didn't we experience His peace when we obeyed?" She knew in her heart the answer was affirmative. Not that they hadn't experienced hardships, and their choices had hardly ever been popular ones. Neither was it this time. But again, after much prayer and seeking counsel, God had opened a way before them.

"Besides, Maryland is sure to have nice things about it too." She bent to gently place her spice cake batter on the rack in the oven.

"It really is a nice day," she decided, as she cleaned up her baking spills. "If I didn't need to finish that rug, I'd do some outside work."

But the truth was, she also enjoyed braiding those rugs. The daughters kept her well supplied with old clothes to cut up into strips. And the $2.00 from each one she sold surely came in handy. She'd never realized as a girl in Ontario that rug braiding was a skill she'd still use so many years later!

On and on her thoughts spun back through the years. The memories weren't all pleasant. Not nearly so. But the years had softened the pain of the worst ones. Perhaps complete harmony was a lifelong quest that was meant to be fulfilled perfectly only when this life was over and the heavenly one begun. Besides, God had blessed her mightily in spite of all the trials. Why should she not thank Him for that?

Susannah's heart nearly overflowed as she considered the riches of God's provisions for her. For the quest had also yielded a security and a trust in the Lord that had become more precious each passing year. Humming before she realized it, she began verbalizing the words to the tune that filled her thoughts.

"Amazing grace! How sweet the sound, that saved a wretch like me! I once was lost, but now I'm found, was blind, but now I see!"

Memory had etched the words deep into her mind. Mentally she could see the notes dance alongside the solemn words. She lifted her voice for the second verse. Then the third. How true were those words written by a stranger even before she was born!

"Through many dangers, toils, and snares, I have already come; 'Twas grace that brought me safe thus far, and grace will lead me home."

Epilogue

John and Susannah did make the move to St. Mary's County, Maryland. While there, they lived next door to their son, Enoch and his family. Those children recall many pleasant memories of helping and being helped by their grandparents in various ways. Listening to stories told by their grandparents was a favorite pastime to the children. Seeds for this story were harvested from memories of long-ago stories shared by John and Susannah.

As they aged and health issues arose, it was decided that they would be cared for by their daughter, Amanda. Once more, John and Susannah moved earthly belongings. This time close to Ephrata, PA., where they spent their last years at the home of Mr. and Mrs. Paul Landis, who lovingly cared for them. Here again, they spent many moments recalling past days, and sharing memories with Paul and Amanda's children. Bits and pieces of those memories, gleaned from the early chapters of their lives were woven into the pages of this book.

John passed away in 1961. Susannah died in 1967. Both were buried at the Stauffer Old Order Mennonite cemetery in Ephrata along Route 322.

Though Susannah often spoke sadly to the grandchildren of the hardships in her life, she didn't harbor resentment toward those who had wronged her. This speaks highly of a born-again Christian life. Neither she nor John were ever able to return to their Canadian birthplace. Letters from there occasionally drifted south, reaching them with news of deaths or events that must surely have pulled at their heart strings.

Bibliography

1. The Heckendorn Family History and Genealogy St. Jacob's printery September, 1971

2. Pleasant Places, © 1997, published at the request of Waterloo-Wellington-Perth Parochial Schools, Wallenstein, Ontario.

3. Martin, Ezra Mennonite Settlement 1887-1915 May City, Iowa Osceola County.

4. Spirit Lake Massacre details are from a personal tour and a tourist pamphlet at the historical museum at Spirit Lake, Iowa.

5. Whistling well incident was taken from archives of the Sibley Gazette, January 9, 1896, Sibley, Iowa. (Copies shared by Alvin Landis.)

6. Copy of John and Susannah's auction fliers, courtesy of the kind ladies at the Tracy House, Ocheyedon, Iowa.

7. Precious Memories of the Groff Family 1935-1994 compiled by Lewis B. and Ella Groff.